Ontario
Probate Kit
David I. Botnick, LAWYER

(a division of)
International Self-Counsel Press Ltd.
Canada   USA

Self-Counsel Press acknowledges the financial support of the Government of Canada through the Canada Book Fund (CBF) for our publishing activities.

Printed in Canada.

First edition: 1976

Tenth edition: 1997; Reprinted 1999

Eleventh edition: 2002

Twelfth edition: 2005; Reprinted: 2008

Thirteenth edition: 2012; Reprinted: 2013

Library and Archives Canada Cataloguing in Publication

Botnick, David I., 1957-

    Ontario probate kit [kit] / David I. Botnick.

    ISBN 978-1-77040-143-3

    1. Probate law and practice—Ontario—Popular works.
2. Probate law and practice—Ontario—Forms. I. Title.

KEO289.B67 2012   346.71305'2   C2012-900624-6
KF765.B67 2012

MIX
Paper from
responsible sources
FSC
www.fsc.org   FSC® C004071

Self-Counsel Press
(a division of)
International Self-Counsel Press Ltd.

North Vancouver, BC   Bellingham, WA
Canada   USA

Contents

Samples

Notice to Readers

Laws are constantly changing. Every effort is made to keep this publication as current as possible. However, the author, the publisher, and the vendor of this book make no representations or warranties regarding the outcome or the use to which the information in this book is put and are not assuming any liability for any claims, losses, or damages arising out of the use of this book. The reader should not rely on the author or the publisher of this book for any professional advice. Please be sure that you have the most recent edition.

Please note, too, that the fees quoted in this book are correct at the date of publication. However, fees are subject to change without notice. For current fees, please check with the court registry nearest you.

Foreword

1. Introduction

The process of probating an estate is primarily a matter of filling out forms and paying close attention to detail. It can be done by anyone with average intelligence who has a little free time. This does not mean to say that the process does not involve some complications — because it does.

Most of the problems are concerned with the information needed to properly complete the forms and the meaning of the actual forms themselves. Depending on where you live, you may also encounter difficulties with certain court or other government personnel. Most are very helpful, but some are not.

In these cases, knowledge of your responsibilities and of the process involved will usually solve the problem.

Why do it yourself? The main reason is, of course, to save money.

Lawyers typically charge between 1.5 and 2 percent of the gross average estate (including the family home) and for small estates this percentage can be as much as 3 percent and higher.

It is not hard to calculate what you save by doing it yourself. And with this book we hope to make the whole process as simple as possible.

You will undoubtedly want to take advantage of the package of forms available from the publisher as it will save a great deal of time in running around. After obtaining the forms, you may proceed immediately to "do it yourself." The whole procedure should be finished in two to three months, even if you are only working on it in your spare time.

A word of advice about using the package of forms and this guide. Do not, as some customers have done, take the forms and the book to the court office and dump them on the counter with a demand that the clerks sort through it all and show you the forms that you are supposed to complete. You will probably get a very rude reception, and deservedly so. Furthermore, such behaviour won't help if you later run into real snags and need a few pointers.

You are far better off to sit down with the book and read it through quickly. Then, refer to those chapters that specifically apply to you. As you read each chapter, note the sample forms you will require for your situation. Note the title of the samples. Remove the matching blank forms from the package and put them aside.

Go slowly through the package. Match up the titles as they appear on the forms and in the book. Use the list that appears in the Table of Contents for quick reference. If you approach the matter in this way, you should experience few problems in selecting the forms that are appropriate for your situation.

2. A Word of Caution: Change in Terminology

On January 1, 1995, the Ontario Court introduced rules that eliminated the use of the terms "Letters Probate" and "Letters of Administration," terms which had been in use for a very long time and with which most people are familiar. These documents are now called "Certificate of Appointment of Estate Trustee with a Will" and "Certificate of Appointment of Estate Trustee without a Will." The terms "probate" and "administration" are still widely used and accepted and will be referred to throughout this book. The new terms are used in Chapters 6 and 7 where the application process for these two different situations is explained.

1

All about Probate

1. What Is Probate Anyway?

The simple definition of probate is the presentation to a court of the will of someone who has died for approval of it as the valid "last will and testament" of the person who made it. Lawmakers are concerned that the true final wishes of a deceased person be acted upon after his or her death. Therefore, they require that a court preside over the distribution of a deceased's assets.

The court also confirms the appointment of the person or persons who have been named in the will to carry out its directions.

If this person is a woman, she is called an executrix in the will. If a man is named, he is called an executor. Their duties are the same. The terms "personal representative" or "estate trustee" include both executor and executrix, and are used interchangeably here.

The personal representative is responsible for what is called the "administration of the estate." Administering the estate means following the deceased person's instructions in distributing and/or managing the estate's assets.

The document issued by the proper court and bearing a legal seal that confirms the validity of the will and the appointment of the personal representative is known as "Certificate of Appointment of Estate Trustee with a Will."

Sometimes problems arise regarding the validity of a will as, for example, where the person who made the will may not have been of a sound mind at the time the will was made. In addition, if it appears that the will was not properly witnessed (in cases where witnesses are required) or that the person who made the will was younger than the age of majority (18 in Ontario), the court will not confirm the will as a valid document. In that case, the estate of the deceased will be handled as though the will had never existed.

If the will is confirmed as being valid, but the named personal representative is younger than the age of majority or is mentally infirm, senile, or generally unable to perform the duties of an executor, the will remains valid and governs the disposition of the deceased's estate. But it is then necessary for the court to name someone to administer the estate according to the provisions of the will.

In most situations, however, these problems do not arise. The will is approved by the court as a valid will and the personal representative named in it is confirmed at the same time.

It should be noted that probate neither validates the will nor affects the appointment of the personal representative named. Probate merely *confirms* the validity of the will of the deceased and *confirms* the appointment(s) already made.

2. Which Court Deals with Probate?

The Superior Court of Justice deals with applications for probate and related estate matters. The Superior Court has court offices in each of the counties, districts, and regional municipalities in Ontario.

All references to the court in this book should be taken to mean the local branch of the Superior Court of Justice.

3. Who Applies and Where?

The application for probate is made to the court of the county, district, or regional municipality in which the deceased has his or her "fixed place of abode" at the time of death.

If the deceased had no permanent home anywhere in Ontario, it is still possible for an application to be made to the court of the county or district in which the deceased had assets or owned property at the time of death.

However, the more common situation is where the deceased died with a permanent residence somewhere in the province of Ontario. In that case, it is only necessary that the location of that residence be found and an application be made to the court in that county, district, or regional municipality.

The application for probate is made by the personal representative named in the will of the deceased. It is not necessary that the forms be completed by a lawyer. In simpler estates there is no reason why the personal representative named cannot successfully fill out the necessary application forms and submit them to the court. The benefit of doing so is, of course, to save the estate the expense of retaining a lawyer.

Applying for probate in Ontario involves filing various documents with the court and paying court fees. Unless questions arise as to the validity of the will or the capacity of the executors to act, *no personal appearance is required in court*.

The various forms are simply completed and submitted to the office of the clerk of the court, where they are checked and the court fees are paid. Once this checking procedure has been completed, the documents are submitted to a judge who formally issues probate. This document is then mailed out to the applicant.

Needless to say, there are various steps throughout the administration of an estate that may require intermittent services by a lawyer. But, when you reach such steps, there is no reason why you cannot retain a lawyer for those specific purposes only.

An example of this is preparing notarized copies of the probate documents. In order to have documents notarized, it is generally necessary for you to appear before a lawyer or a notary public.

If there are beneficiaries named in the will who have not reached the age of majority (18 in Ontario), the administration of the estate may prove too difficult for a lay person.

The complication in this case is that the share of the estate that has been left to anyone younger than the age of majority cannot be paid to him or her at that time but must be held in trust by the personal representative or in court (depending on the provisions of the will) until the child turns 18.

The administration of an estate will require organization, common sense, and an understanding of the concepts that are set out in this book. The purpose of the book is not to enable everyone who reads it to be able to handle every estate that comes along. Rather, this book sets out in a straightforward manner the various steps required for the successful probate of an estate and the disposition of the assets to the rightful beneficiaries.

As a point of interest, approximately 85 percent of the estates probated are relatively simple, so the chances are that yours will fall into this category.

As mentioned, there are, of course, certain instances where it is advisable to obtain legal advice concerning the distribution of the estate. An example would be where there is a dispute involving the validity of the will or the gifts made under it.

Such disputes often lead to lawsuits. It would probably be inadvisable for you to attempt to handle this sort of situation on your own.

In cases where the estate involves the transferring of property which at the time of death is situated outside the province of Ontario, it would probably be advisable for you to retain a lawyer to ensure that the provisions of the foreign jurisdiction (that is, the other province or country) are properly observed.

There may well be death taxes or duties payable in that foreign jurisdiction. There may also be documents that need to be filed with the other government in question.

4. Why Apply for Probate?

Probating an estate confirms the validity of the will and the appointment of the executor or executrix named in it. It is possible, however, in very simple estates, to avoid any necessity to probate the will at all.

If the assets are small in number and small in value, it is quite possible for the administration to be carried out without application being made. For example, where the estate consists only of a car and a bank account in the name of the deceased person, the car can be transferred readily without probate.

Also, it is often possible to convince a bank to transfer a bank account by providing *suitable indemnities* (guarantees) and by showing a notarial copy of the will. (A notarial copy is one that has been sworn to as a true copy by a notary public.)

Unfortunately, it is impossible to say just exactly how small is small for purposes of avoiding probate. Really, it depends on the disposition of the person or persons in charge of transferring the various assets. For example, transferring a car is easy and this can be done by simply showing an official at a motor vehicle transfer office a notarial copy of the will and death certificate.

Similarly, a small insurance policy and bank account should be no problem. But Government of Canada bonds or stocks and bonds of public companies would be very difficult to transfer without producing the forms proving that probate had been obtained.

If you are in doubt as to your situation, the simple answer is to pick up the phone and call the various officials in charge of these transfers and see what they say.

Remember, the reason for obtaining probate is to satisfy third parties and to prove you are entitled to deal with the assets of the deceased person. In other words, the court approval given to the will serves as evidence to the world that the personal representative is who he or she claims to be and that the disposition of the deceased's assets is done according to law.

Quite often, strangers are reluctant to deal with a person claiming to be a personal representative under the provisions of a will that has not been probated simply because they do not want to take the risk that the will may be invalid or the appointment of the personal representative may prove not to be proper. For this reason, it is possible in only the very simplest of estates to avoid the necessity of applying for probate.

You will readily see that the best reason for obtaining probate is to enable the personal representative to deal as easily as possible with the assets of the estate and arrange their transfer to the rightful beneficiaries.

This book cannot possibly deal with all the questions that may arise during the handling of an estate, but it will enable you to handle most of the common transfers and to understand the whole process.

In most cases, it will also permit you to probate an estate yourself. It is hoped, as well, that the book will have the effect of indicating when it would be advisable to seek legal advice.

Finally, it should be pointed out that the clerks in the court offices are, generally speaking, very helpful and are prepared to assist in the completion of forms although they are not allowed to fill in the forms for you. You should not hesitate to seek the advice of these individuals if you have any questions that are not answered by this book.

2

What Do You Do As an Executor?

1. Introduction

If you are named in the will of the deceased to administer the deceased's estate, you are an executor or executrix (also called a personal representative or estate trustee).

By statute law, you have certain powers and corresponding obligations and responsibilities in handling the estate. You are also a "trustee" and are bound by all of the provisions of the *Trustee Act* (Ontario).

The person making a will, known as the testator (or testatrix if a woman), can restrict or enlarge the powers of his or her personal representative by inserting various clauses in the will.

This book attempts to set forth the more common powers, obligations, and responsibilities. While reading it, however, bear in mind that the provisions of the will with which you are dealing may change the general rules. Obviously, one of your first duties is to become fully familiar with the will in question.

This book is not intended to cover the subject of drafting wills. If you wish to pursue that area in some detail, you should obtain a copy of *Write Your Legal Will in 3 Easy Steps*, another title in the Self-Counsel series, where you will find a detailed and simplified discussion of the various provisions that may be inserted into a will.

2. What General Requirements Must You Meet?

In order to be appointed by the court, you must be at least 18 years of age. As well, if you are appointed by the will, you will not be eligible and will not be confirmed by the court if you are unable mentally or physically to perform the necessary duties.

It should also be pointed out that unless you are a resident of Canada or another Commonwealth country, a bond must be posted as security with the court for the proper performance of the duties undertaken. This bond will generally be the same as that required for an administrator.

As will be noted in the next chapter, all administrators are required to post a bond unless special dispensation is obtained. Such special dispensation is also available for a "foreign executor" (i.e., one not resident in Canada or elsewhere in the Commonwealth).

Please refer to the next chapter for a discussion of the requirements for a bond and the situations in which it can be dispensed with.

As long as you are resident in Canada or elsewhere in the Commonwealth, no bond is required and no special dispensation need be sought.

3. What Are Your Powers?

You have, by law, legal title to all of the assets of the deceased person. This means that you have the capacity to transfer them to the beneficiaries named in the will.

If the will grants you the power to sell any or all of the assets or property and distribute the cash instead, you have the power to carry out such sales as may be necessary.

If it is necessary to sell some of the assets of the estate in order to pay debts of the deceased or death taxes, you have the power to sell such assets as are necessary even when there is no specific provision contained in the will. You must not sell any assets specifically bequeathed to a named beneficiary unless there are not sufficient additional assets other than those named in the will.

You have access to all personal effects of the deceased and may take possession of them. You also have the capacity to accept money owing to the deceased or to pay debts owing by the deceased at the time of death.

4. What Are Your Duties and Responsibilities?

A checklist of the various duties of an executor is in the appendix.

Generally, it is your duty to file all income tax returns of the deceased and the estate (if applicable), to pay all the debts of the estate, and to take title to the assets of the deceased and transfer them to the proper beneficiaries.

One of your first duties is to arrange for the burial of the deceased. This obligation will undoubtedly arise before any application for probate has even been considered.

This is where the legal theory that you, as executor, take your power from the will rather than from filing for probate becomes significant. It is not necessarily the surviving spouse of the deceased person who has the right and duty to arrange for the funeral, although it is often assumed that this is so. This is the case only if the surviving spouse also happens to be the personal representative appointed in the will.

In the eyes of the law, you are the one who "has property in the body" and therefore makes the decisions about the funeral arrangements!

You have the power to incur reasonable funeral expenses and to pay these expenses out of the assets of the estate. If an excessive amount is spent on the funeral, the beneficiaries of the estate may go to court to question your right to incur such large debts and, if the court determines the amount spent to be unreasonable, you may be liable to reimburse the estate for those portions of the estate that were spent and that were considered excessive.

The determination of whether funeral expenses were reasonable or not depends on the deceased's position in life and the size of his or her estate. Obviously, it is impossible to lay down hard and fast rules about this. It is basically up to your common sense to ensure that the expenses are reasonable in the circumstances.

If you are in some doubt as to whether or not expenses are reasonable, and if all of the beneficiaries of the estate are over the age of 18, it would be a wise precaution to obtain their written consents or agreements to the cost of funeral arrangements.

Once you possess these consents, it would be very difficult for the beneficiaries to question the expenditures at a later date.

It is also your duty to become fully familiar with the affairs of the estate and the assets and liabilities of the deceased.

Ultimately, your duty is to distribute the estate to the beneficiaries named in the will and to account to them for the handling of the funds and assets of the estate.

You are responsible for your actions during the administration of the estate and accountable at all times to the beneficiaries who may question your conduct before the court.

It should be made clear that it is possible for more than one executor to be acting at the same time in the administration of an estate. Often a will names two or even three executors to act at the same time. This is perfectly permissible.

However, if it does occur, each of them must be sure to be fully aware of what the others are doing with the assets of the estate. Each executor is responsible for the actions of the co-executors. Thus, if you are a co-executor, it becomes extremely important for you to know what the other co-executor is doing.

In a situation where there is more than one executor acting at once, it is necessary for them to be unanimous in any decision in order to function. This rule can be qualified by a provision in the will which indicates that a majority decision will govern.

Finally, it should be pointed out that in a situation where there is more than one personal representative appointed and probate is taken out by them, in the event of the death of one of them, the survivors have the power to carry on automatically. There is no need to replace the deceased executor nor are the powers of the surviving executors limited by the death.

You cannot delegate your position to another person although you can refuse the responsibility in the first place. Simply because you are named in the will as executor does not mean that you are obliged to take on the role.

You may "renounce" or indicate that you are not prepared to take on the responsibility of the position of personal representative by filling out a "renunciation" form which can be filed with the probate papers at the court.

Usually there is a co-executor involved in these situations and it is no problem. If you are a sole executor and renounce or if, say, two co-executors resign, the estate then comes under the rules of administration (with will annexed).

Sample 1 shows the form used to renounce probate. The form must be signed in the presence of a witness who then signs his or her name on the line indicated.

The will may contain a provision permitting you to appoint a replacement. In such a situation, the provision of the will governs rather than the general rule stated above.

5. What about the Payment of the Debts of the Estate?

Although there is no obligation for you to advertise for creditors, it has become the practice in most situations to do so. You are well advised to publish in a local newspaper a "Notice to creditors and others" who may have a claim against the estate. An example of such a notice can be found in Sample 2.

The advertisement will protect you from claims made against you for outstanding debts of the deceased after all of the assets have been distributed to the beneficiaries.

Needless to say, this would be a very awkward position for you to be in and one that can be avoided by an advertisement for creditors.

The practice has developed of having the notice inserted on three separate occasions, the insertions being one week apart. The notice should be placed in a newspaper published in the region where the deceased lived prior to death. Therefore, you will save money by placing such an advertisement in a local newspaper as opposed to one with a wider circulation.

The notice itself will provide for a date by which all claims against the estate must be filed with you, failing which the assets will be distributed having regard only to the claims then known.

SAMPLE 1
RENUNCIATION OF RIGHT TO A CERTIFICATE OF APPOINTMENT OF
ESTATE TRUSTEE WITH A WILL

FORM 74.11

Courts of Justice Act

RENUNCIATION OF RIGHT TO A CERTIFICATE OF APPOINTMENT OF ESTATE TRUSTEE
(OR SUCCEEDING ESTATE TRUSTEE) WITH A WILL

ONTARIO   *(Court file no.)*

SUPERIOR COURT OF JUSTICE

IN THE ESTATE OF   JOHN EDWARD JONES   , deceased.
                                              (insert name)

**RENUNCIATION OF RIGHT TO A CERTIFICATE OF APPOINTMENT OF ESTATE TRUSTEE
(OR SUCCEEDING ESTATE TRUSTEE) WITH A WILL**

The deceased died on _____ JANUARY 20, 20-- _____ *(date)*.

In that person's testamentary document dated _____ NOVEMBER 15, 20-- _____ *(date)*, I, _____ JENNIFER JONES _____
(insert name), was named an estate trustee.

I renounce my right to a certificate of appointment of estate trustee (or succeeding estate trustee) with a will.

DATE   FEBRUARY 23, 20--

)
)
)
)
...........*I.M. Witness*...........   )   ....*Jennifer Jones*...........
Signature of witness   )   Signature of person renouncing
)
)
)

RCP-E 74.11 (November 1, 2005)
SELF-COUNSEL PRESS-PROBATE-ONT (FORM 74.11) (7-1)07

SAMPLE 2
NOTICE TO CREDITORS AND OTHERS

NOTICE TO CREDITORS AND OTHERS

IN THE ESTATE OF JOHN ADAMS SMITH, late of 42 Rose Avenue in the City of Toronto, in the Province of Ontario.

ALL PERSONS having claims against the estate of JOHN ADAMS SMITH, late of 42 Rose Avenue in the City of Toronto who died on or about the 1st day of March 20--, are hereby required to send full particulars of such claims to the undersigned executrix on or before the 28th day of May, 20-- after which date the estate's assets will be distributed having regard only to claims that have then been received and the undersigned will not be liable to any person of whose claim she shall not then have notice.

Dated at Toronto this 3rd day of April 20--

MARY MATILDA SMITH
42 Rose Avenue
Toronto, Ontario

There is no set time to allow creditors to reply to the advertisement, but the date chosen should obviously be several weeks after the publication of the third insertion.

The important point to note here is that the advertisement is placed for the protection of you and not the creditors. It is rare that a creditor ever sees this type of advertisement but, without it, you could later be held personally responsible for the unpaid debt. Basically it is up to you to decide whether or not an advertisement should be placed.

You should carefully check each claim that is submitted to the estate. If at all unsure of its validity, you should require proof that the deceased did incur the debt and that it has not already been paid. Such proof can be obtained in the form of invoices, letters, or order forms.

You should be able to establish whether payment has been made by a review of the bank account of the deceased person. If all else fails, the creditor can be required to sign and swear an affidavit stating his or her right to payment in order to give you some reliable document to justify payment of the claimed amount.

6. What Do You Do When There Is an Appointment of a Lawyer in the Will?

From time to time, a will prepared either by an individual or by his or her lawyer will contain a provision that purports to appoint a certain lawyer or law firm to act as the estate's lawyer after the death of the person making the will.

Sometimes this appointment takes the form of a direction to the personal representative to employ a certain lawyer.

It should be pointed out that the Law Society of Upper Canada has ruled such a practice to be objectionable as being a form of solicitation for business. Nevertheless, the provision will be found from time to time in older wills and sometimes in more recent wills.

Not only is the practice objectionable but, generally speaking, it is not one that binds you. The general rule is that the lawyer (if any) is retained by you and not by the deceased. You have the power under law to retain legal protection and assistance if desired. Thus, you, as personal representative, are given the right to choose whomever you wish as a lawyer.

Courts over the years have ruled that the purported appointment in the will of a lawyer to act for the estate is not enforceable.

It would undoubtedly be a good idea to contact any lawyer so named and advise him or her that you do not wish him or her to act and to obtain an acknowledgment in writing that this is acceptable and that there will be no claim to any entitlement for legal fees or damages for not being retained as the estate lawyer.

This is probably not an essential step but might be extra insurance for you if you are facing a will that contains such an appointment.

7. What Can You Charge?

Under the law of the province of Ontario, you are entitled as a matter of course to a reasonable fee for services rendered in the administration of an estate.

You are, of course, entitled as well to be reimbursed for any monies spent in the performance of your duties. This reimbursement is subject to the rule of reasonableness, as you are not entitled to spend amounts of money that cannot be seen as necessary and reasonable in the circumstances of the particular estate.

There are no written rules as to the exact amount of compensation to which you are entitled for the administration of an estate. However, rules of thumb have been developed which are based on the value of the assets of the estate. These rules of thumb are not hard and fast and are subject to regional variances.

Personal representatives are generally entitled to a fee of 5 percent of the gross value of the assets of the estate for supervising the probate and distribution of the assets.

If the estate is a more complicated one involving services stretching over a number of years, such as the investment of assets and the collection of income and payment out to beneficiaries, you are also entitled to 5 percent of the income collected by the estate and paid out to beneficiaries.

In some areas, you will also be awarded a management fee per year in estates involving substantial investments retained over a period of years. A common figure used by the courts is 0.4 percent per annum on the gross value of the estate.

However the total compensation is arrived at, and whatever components are used in calculating it, it should be made clear that the compensation is payable to you as a group.

In other words, if more than one is serving, the compensation is the same as it would have been had there been only one personal representative. In a situation where there is more than one personal representative, it is up to all of you to arrange for the division of the compensation between you.

If a dispute as to the division should arise, this can be settled on an application to the court.

Note: In cases where you are also a beneficiary, it is more beneficial tax-wise for you to take from the estate as a beneficiary. Income from being a personal representative is taxable as income but the receipt by a beneficiary of assets of an estate does not result in taxation.

8. What Can a Lawyer Charge?

A lawyer handling an estate and acting for the personal representative is also entitled to compensation out of the assets of the estate. This compensation is based on the value of the estate, the professional skill required, and the time involved. Although there are no fixed prices for lawyers' fees for probating an estate, the scale of fees recommended by the Toronto Law Association for an estate of average complexity is as follows:

(a) On the first $100,000 of the value of the estate or a portion thereof, 3 percent of the amount

(b) On the next $400,000 or portion thereof, 1.25 percent of the amount

(c) On the next $500,000 or portion thereof, 0.5 percent of the amount

(d) On the excess over $1,000,000, additional fees may be charged on the basis of the time involved, the result achieved, and the value of the estate.

The above scale of fees is not followed by all lawyers. By careful shopping, you can probably locate a competent lawyer who will handle the estate for a smaller fee. Of course you will save even more money if you decide to do the work yourself and seek a lawyer's advice only when it is needed.

Legal fees charged in estate administration are, like any legal fees, subject to review by a court-appointed assessment officer upon application by the person charged. In addition, there is provision for a judge of the court to review both the lawyer's and the personal representative's account.

3

What Do You Do As an Administrator?

1. What Are the Differences between an Executor and an Administrator?

An executor is appointed by the will of a deceased person to handle the administration of that person's estate; an administrator is appointed by the court to handle an estate where the deceased did not leave a will.

The procedure of probating an estate is merely the confirmation of the appointment of the person named in a will. However, in situations where it is necessary for the court to appoint an individual to handle the administration of an estate, the name given to the person is administrator (or administratrix, if a woman).

Both executors and administrators are also called personal representatives or estate trustees. Generally, the duties, rights, and obligations are much the same.

The appointment of an administrator by the court is required where a person dies without leaving any will at all. This is known as dying "intestate."

In such a circumstance, an application is made to the court for "Certificate of Appointment of Estate Trustee without a Will."

Because there is no will, the administrator, once appointed, has no statement from the will to guide him or her in the disposition of the property of the deceased.

Therefore, an administrator must resort to the statutes. The *Succession Law Reform Act* determines the distribution of the estate of a person dying intestate. The administrator, rather than distributing the assets of the estate in accordance with a will, distributes those assets according to the provincial law.

2. Who Can Apply for Administration?

Generally speaking, the nearest relative of the deceased person applies for administration. Where there is more than one applicant, the court will generally choose the nearest next-of-kin.

The court makes the decision as to who will be the administrator. In a situation where there is a surviving spouse, the claim of the spouse will usually have first priority. The right to be so appointed, however, is generally applied in the following order:

(a) Spouse

(b) Child or children

(c) Grandchildren

(d) Parent

(e) Brothers or sisters

(f) Nephews or nieces

Although it is technically possible to have more than one administrator act at the same time, the court usually favours single administrators.

If there are no applicants, a provincial official named the Public Guardian and Trustee has the power under provincial law to apply and administrate the estate.

Interestingly enough, even a creditor of the deceased has a sufficient interest to apply for the appointment as administrator. However, it is unlikely that his or her application would be accepted in a case where any of the next-of-kin of the deceased person makes a similar application.

In any situation where there is a person with a prior or equal right to apply for administration, a renunciation should be signed by such a person or persons and submitted to the court with the other documents in connection with the application (see Chapter 7).

3. What Can You Do before You Are Officially Appointed As the Administrator?

An application for administration will not be accepted by the court until at least 14 days after the death of the deceased person.

The difficulty in this situation is that, while an executor obtains his or her power from the will and is in a position to act immediately upon the death of the deceased person, an administrator cannot, simply because no one knows who the administrator is going to be immediately following the death of the deceased.

This creates practical problems when it comes to making funeral arrangements. As was discussed in the previous chapter, the executor is the one with the power to incur funeral expenses and with the duty to arrange for the burial of the deceased.

Who, then, in a situation where there is no will or in a situation where there is a will but no one named as executor, can make the necessary arrangements for expenses out of the estate?

It is quite clear that an administrator has absolutely no authority until appointed by the court. Worse still, the appointment is not retroactive and does not date back to the date of the death.

In most cases this should not become a problem because the beneficiaries (members of the family) can usually agree beforehand about who should apply to become the administrator.

In any event, it is still advisable to act very cautiously in such situations, especially when substantial funeral expenses may be incurred. In other words, you should ensure that these expenditures are, at all times, reasonable.

As a practical matter, few expenses are refused reimbursement by administrators later, but if you act without any authority and incur expenses that you hope the estate will pay at a later date, you should bear in mind this warning.

Obviously, none of the assets of the deceased should be distributed or sold until administration is obtained. Until then, no one has the right or the power to deal with any of the deceased's assets.

Practically speaking, of course, someone will have to take custody and possession of many of the assets of the deceased person. These should merely be retained "in trust" until a court appointment is obtained.

This means that the self-appointed administrator should be very careful in keeping records and ensuring there is no mixing of funds or assets with his or her own or with anyone else's.

The problem of debts should not arise in the normal situation. There are very few debts that will require payment before administration is obtained. Usually, creditors understand the situation and will be patient until that time.

If any of the assets of the deceased person are either sold or distributed or used to pay debts before administration is complete, the person interfering with these assets runs the risk of being personally accountable to the next-of-kin if any damage or financial loss results to the estate.

4. Are There Any Residency Requirements?

Only people resident in the province of Ontario may apply for administration.

Accordingly, if there is no person in the province of Ontario eligible for appointment, it may be necessary to nominate a lawyer or trust company in Ontario to act as administrator of the estate.

An alternative to this is to permit the Public Guardian and Trustee to apply for administration.

5. Are There Any Requirements for a Bond?

Reference was made earlier to the requirement of a bond in certain situations where a personal representative named in the will applies for probate.

Under the provisions of the *Estates Act*, anyone applying for administration is required first to post security with the court. This security usually takes the form of a bond and the general requirement is an amount that is twice the amount of the value of the assets of the estate listed on the inventory for court purposes.

It is then necessary to obtain two sureties (i.e., two individuals who will post the bond in order to satisfy the court). The sureties must be in a position not only to post the bond, but also to swear that they have sufficient assets in their names to cover the amount that they have posted. Where the value of the estate is $5,000 or less, one surety is sufficient.

The more common way of handling the bond is to apply to one of several bonding companies which are in the business of providing security in such situations.

In such a case, the court will accept a bond in the amount of the estate (rather than in an amount twice the value of the estate) and will accept just one bonding company as surety.

This bond is purchased on the basis of an annual premium after the filing of an application form and is based on the creditworthiness of the executor as well as the value of the estate.

The procedure can be compared to the purchase of an insurance policy. A typical bond for a period of one year to cover an estate worth $100,000 would cost about $400. Bonding companies can be readily located in the Yellow Pages telephone directory or through your insurance broker.

There is provision in the *Estates Act* for a reduction of or complete dispensation with the bond. Normally an application for administration must be accompanied by the bond or it will not be accepted by the court. If you desire to dispense with the bond completely or to have it reduced, you are required to file an affidavit setting out the circumstances supporting your request.

Although the legislation does not spell out specifically the circumstances in which a bond will be dispensed with, the practice has developed of granting an order dispensing with the bond in a situation where all of the next-of-kin who are to benefit under the estate consent to the applicant's acting without a bond, and where all of those next-of-kin are 18 or older.

Due to the fact that the bond is also intended to protect creditors as well as next-of-kin, it is necessary for evidence to be filed with the court establishing that all of the creditors of the estate have been paid as well. If the necessary material is provided to the judge, he or she will issue an order dispensing with the requirement of the administrator's bond.

As stated in the previous chapter, similar rules apply to "foreign executors." In the same way that an administrator's bond can be dispensed with or reduced, so too can a foreign executor's bond be dispensed with or reduced.

The *Estates Act* also provides that where there is no will and the estate has a value of $200,000 or less and where the applicant for administration is the surviving spouse of the deceased, if he or she files an affidavit with the court confirming that all of the debts of the estate have been paid, administration can be obtained without the requirement to obtain an order from a judge dispensing with the bond. (An example of this affidavit is shown in Sample 21 in Chapter 7.)

The reason for this is simply that, in such circumstances, the whole of the estate passes to the widow or widower in any event.

The scope of this book is such that any further discussion of the procedure for dispensing with a bond would not be appropriate. If you become involved in such a situation, you are advised to retain legal counsel at least for this particular portion of the estate administration.

6. What Are Your Powers, Duties, and Obligations As an Administrator?

Although there are differences, some minor and some more significant, between the powers, duties, and obligations of administrators and those of executors, in the average estate it is generally safe to say that the powers, duties, and obligations are much the same.

7. What about Distribution of an Estate When There Is No Will?

In the situation where there is no will, the distribution is governed by the *Succession Law Reform Act*. In such circumstances it may be advisable to obtain legal advice to ensure that the assets are being distributed properly, especially if you fear some dispute over the estate.

The administrator who acts mistakenly could be held personally liable for any losses suffered by the heirs who were unjustly deprived of a portion of the estate.

The actual distribution of an estate in the case of an intestacy will depend in every case on what relatives and next-of-kin survive the deceased. I recommend highly that some legal advice be obtained at this stage to ensure that the assets are properly distributed.

The scheme of distribution under the *Succession Law Reform Act* results in different allocations of an estate depending on the circumstances, and you should ensure that the proper set of rules is applied in the administration of any intestate's estate.

8. Division under the *Succession Law Reform Act*

The rules that follow are to be applied in all cases where the deceased died without a will.

8.1 Death of a married person with issue

The rules that govern widows and widowers are under the *Succession Law Reform Act*.

(a) A surviving spouse will take the first $200,000 of the net value of the estate. In addition, if the couple had one child, the surviving spouse will also take one-half of the residue (that is, the amount in excess of $200,000) and the child will take the other half. If more than one child exists, the surviving spouse will take one-third of the excess over $200,000, the remaining two-thirds being divided equally between the children.

(b) Where some but not all of the children of the deceased die before the parent, their children (in other words, the grandchildren of the intestate) will share equally the share of their deceased parent.

(c) If all of the children of the intestate have died before their parent, the portion of the estate that does not pass to the surviving spouse is divided equally among the grandchildren, no matter how many children the deceased had.

The law relating to representation by children of deceased issue can be complex. You should seek legal counsel before attempting a distribution in any such situation.

8.2 Death of a person with issue but no spouse

(a) If either a man or a woman dies leaving no spouse but leaving one child, the whole of the estate will pass to the one surviving child.

(b) In the event of such a death where two or more children survive, the entire estate is divided equally among the surviving children.

(c) Where some but not all of the children of the deceased have died before the parent, their children (in other words, the grandchildren of the intestate) will share equally their parents' share.

(d) If all of the children of the intestate have died before the parent, the estate is divided equally among the grandchildren, no matter how many children the deceased had.

Again, you are warned of the complexities involved when representation of deceased heirs is involved.

8.3 Death of a person with spouse but no issue

Under the *Succession Law Reform Act*, if there are no issue alive at the time of the death of the intestate, the surviving spouse is entitled to the whole estate.

8.4 Death of a person with no spouse and no issue

The *Succession Law Reform Act* creates a scheme of distribution of structure. The first five classes are as follows:

Class one: father, mother

Class two: brothers, sisters

Class three: nephews, nieces

Class four: grandmother, grandfather

Class five: uncles, aunts

The estate is divided equally among all members of the closest class of next-of-kin. As long as there is at least one next-of-kin living in the closest class, that single individual will inherit the whole estate. No other next-of-kin in a more distant class regardless of the number that may exist will receive any benefits under the *Succession Law Reform Act*.

As an example, if a man left no spouse or issue and was survived by his mother (his father having died), the whole estate would pass to the mother irrespective of whether there were any other living relatives in any of the higher (more distant) classes.

9. What Is Escheat?

If an intestate leaves no spouse, descendants, or other blood relatives, under the laws of Ontario all of his or her property will pass to the provincial government. This concept is known as "escheat."

This will occur only where there is no spouse, and there are no descendants, and no blood relatives whatsoever.

Although the situation does not arise very frequently, it does happen from time to time that an estate does "escheat" to the provincial crown.

4

Legal Recognition of Illegitimacy and Dependants' Rights

This chapter deals with three unrelated matters:

(a) The rights of surviving spouses

(b) The recognition of illegitimate relatives for the purposes of inheritance either of an intestacy or through the provisions of a will

(c) A deceased's obligations to his or her "dependants"

These matters will be of concern if you are attempting to administer an estate.

1. The Rights of Surviving Spouses

Under the *Family Law Act*, a surviving spouse is given additional rights above those set out in the *Succession Law Reform Act*. The purpose of these rights is to ensure that a spouse whose marriage partner dies has at least the same rights as a spouse whose partner leaves because of a separation or divorce.

In the case of a separation or divorce, each spouse is generally entitled to receive one half of the total family property acquired during the marriage. Similarly, when a spouse dies, the surviving spouse may claim one half of the family property acquired by the spouses during the marriage. The right to make this claim exists even where the deceased has made a will leaving nothing to his or her spouse. However, the application to court to make the claim must be made no later than six months after the deceased spouse's death.

When a spouse dies leaving a will, the surviving spouse must choose between taking the share left to him or her under the will or making a claim for half of the family property under the *Family Law Act*. If there is no will, the surviving spouse must choose between his or her entitlement under the *Succession Law Reform Act* (see section 8. in Chapter 3) or making a claim under the *Family Law Act*.

This choice is known as an "election." The election should be made in writing within six months from the date of the spouse's death and delivered to the executor or administrator. It should also be filed at the office of the Estate Registrar for Ontario.

In the case of a typical will where each spouse leaves his or her entire estate to the surviving spouse, the election to claim under the *Family Law Act* is of no value since the spouse is going to receive the entire estate under the terms of the will. However, if your spouse has left a will in which you do not inherit the entire estate, or if your spouse dies intestate, you should seek legal advice to determine whether a claim under the *Family Law Act* should be made.

The executor or administrator of a deceased spouse's estate may not distribute any assets of the estate within six months of the spouse's death unless the surviving spouse gives written consent to the distribution or it is authorized by the court. The reason for this is to allow the surviving spouse time to bring a claim under the *Family Law Act* if he or she elects to do so.

If you are the personal representative of an estate in which there is a surviving spouse, a claim under the *Family Law Act* could drastically change the distribution of the estate. You should, therefore, always seek the written consent of the spouse before making any distribution of the estate. If you cannot obtain the spouse's consent, you should seek legal advice to be sure that the *Family Law Act* has not been contravened. If the spouse has notified you that he or she is claiming entitlement under the *Family Law Act*, the estate will require legal representation.

2. Recognition of Children and Other Relatives Born Out of Marriage

The *Succession Law Reform* Act equates children born within a marriage and children born outside of marriage as well as children born of a common-law relationship. Both are treated alike for the purposes of the distribution of the estate of a person dying intestate. This applies in the case of both a deceased mother and a deceased father. In fact, the legislation goes further.

Accordingly, if a nephew born within a marriage and a nephew born outside marriage were the only heirs, they would share equally in the estate of their intestate uncle or aunt.

The rules that equate heirs born within marriage and outside marriage apply both in the case of an intestacy and in the case where a will is left. In the case of a will, however, it is possible for a person to exclude the relation born outside of marriage by expressly stating this in the will. Specific words must be included in any will if any such relatives are to be precluded from receiving benefits under that will.

Thus, if a testator had four children of a marriage and a fifth child from a relationship outside of that marriage, simply leaving assets to be divided equally among his or her children would result in a division into five equal parts, the fifth child sharing equally with the other children. In order to avoid this, it is necessary to indicate in a will that you wish only your children born within your marriage to be considered when the division is made.

Note: The rules including heirs born outside of marriage will only apply to any will made on or after March 31, 1978. If a will is dated prior to that time, it will be interpreted in accordance with the old laws which would omit "illegitimate" heirs.

It is anticipated that there may be some difficulty in establishing if a claimant is or is not the child of the parent in question. The legislation casts an obligation on the personal representative to make reasonable inquiries for people who may be entitled to a share of the estate as a result of a relationship traced through a birth outside of marriage. In the case of large families where benefits are being left to relatives more distant than children, such inquiries might be difficult to make.

Where relatives born outside marriage may be eligible to inherit, the personal representative is obliged to carry out the necessary investigations to ensure that there are no such relatives in the class or group named in a will or inheriting on an intestacy. Do not assume that none exists. The apparently embarrassing question will have to be put to all those who might have knowledge of such things. This group should certainly include the deceased's family, doctor, and lawyer.

In addition to questioning the deceased's friends and relatives, the personal representative should also search the records of parentage at the office of the Registrar General of Ontario. This office maintains an index of fathers who complete a declaration of paternity when a child is born or who were the subject of a finding of paternity by a court.

It is important to make such inquiries, for if the estate is distributed without regard for this obligation, the personal representative may be held personally liable to any heir who subsequently surfaces claiming his or her share.

3. The Rights of a Dependant

Traditionally, a person making a will was permitted complete discretion in deciding who would inherit his or her estate. This concept is referred to as "testamentary freedom." We have already seen that this concept has been limited by the case of surviving spouses.

The *Succession Law Reform Act* provides a further limitation by allowing anyone who qualifies as a "dependant" of the deceased to bring a claim for financial support from the estate. In addition to a spouse being entitled to bring an application, the legislation includes both a common-law spouse and a former spouse within the definition of "dependant." It is from this part of the *Succession Law Reform Act* that the common-law spouse now gets some protection on the death of the other common-law spouse, protection that did not exist before. The common-law spouse still is not included in the distribution on an intestacy. His or her protection comes, however, from an ability to challenge the distribution in the case of an intestacy or under a will if he or she is not properly provided for. "Common-law spouse" is defined as either a man or a woman not married to each other who have been cohabiting continuously for a period of not less than three years immediately prior to the death of one of them, or who have been cohabiting in a relationship of some permanence in which a child has been born to them.

The inclusion of a former spouse in the law means if the deceased was providing support or was under a legal obligation to provide support immediately before death to a former spouse from whom he or she was divorced, such former spouse qualifies as a "dependant."

The definition of "dependant" also includes, in addition to children (of any age), grandchildren, brothers, sisters, and even parents and grandparents of the deceased if the deceased was providing support or was under a legal obligation to provide support to that person immediately before death.

For the purposes of a support application, children include not only natural children of the deceased, but also anyone whom the deceased has demonstrated a settled intention to treat as a child of his or her family. A step-son or step-daughter would therefore be entitled in most cases to apply as a dependant in the estate of a step-father or step-mother.

These support obligations of the *Succession Law Reform Act* can be invoked by a dependant whether there is a will or not. Thus, it is possible, for example, for a daughter of the deceased to be entitled to a certain share of her father's estate on an intestacy and yet to bring an application based on the argument that the share to which she became entitled was not enough and that she should also be awarded more from the share of some other relative inheriting on the intestacy, perhaps even her mother.

A dependant can bring an application before the court where the deceased has not made "adequate provision for the proper support" of the dependant. Section 62 of the act sets forth a lengthy list of matters a court should consider on an application to determine what allowance should be granted to the dependant out of the estate of the deceased. These include obvious factors such as the dependant's assets and means, age, capacity to provide for his or her own support, accustomed standard of living, the proximity and duration of the relationship between the dependant and the deceased, and, where the dependant is a child older than the age of 16, his or her withdrawal from parental control. A number of other matters for the court to consider are set out in the act. The legislation has not attempted to define "adequate provision for the proper support" but has only given the court some guidelines to assist it. The many cases decided under previous legislation should continue to be of assistance as precedents for applications under the Succession Law Reform Act.

It is virtually impossible to predict with any certainty the amount that the court will order as an allowance to a successful applicant. Although there were many decided cases under the former legislation, each case is different and must be decided on its own facts. The judge is given very broad discretion under the act to decide upon the form and the amount of the allowance awarded to the dependant.

Applications under the *Succession Law Reform Act* are made to the court of the county or judicial district in which the deceased had a fixed place of abode at the time of his or her death. Thus, if the deceased person did not live in Ontario, no application by a dependant is possible under the act, even by a dependant who lives in Ontario. Most of the other provinces and many other countries have similar (but not identical) legislation. If the deceased lived in, say, Manitoba, at the time of death, the dependant would then be governed by the Manitoba legislation rather than by the *Succession Law Reform Act*.

Under the Act, an application may be brought within six months after probate or administration. A further extension of the period may be allowed by the court if it considers it proper, but any such late application can only affect any portion of the estate which has not already been distributed.

If the court grants an application by a dependant, the Act provides for a broad range of possible orders. The court may order the estate to make periodic, annual or otherwise, payments to the dependant for an indefinite period or for a limited number of years or until the happening of a certain event. It would appear possible, for example, for an order to be made in favour of a spouse or common-law spouse until he or she remarried. Or, to take another example, an order could be made in favour of a dependant in school until he or she graduated or left university. A lump sum payment is also permitted. In addition, the court may order a specific asset or article to be transferred to the successful applicant. Also, the court may order the use of any specified property for life or for a limited time. As you can see, the court has an extremely wide discretion as to the type of order it can make. This should enable the court to meet almost any kind of situation. The most common type of award has traditionally been the periodic payment, although lump sum awards are made where periodic payments would unduly delay the winding-up of the estate.

The *Succession Law Reform Act* also provides for a re-hearing at a subsequent date, permitting the court to vary, discharge, or suspend any order previously made by it or to inquire into the adequacy of any order previously made by it. Thus if, after an award is made, the fortunes of the dependant improve, a further application could be brought by the beneficiaries of the estate (out of whose share the order was made) to have the payments reduced or even terminated, thereby restoring to them their full share of the estate.

Under the Act, joint accounts and life insurance proceeds paid under policies owned by the deceased are also available to be charged for the benefit of a dependant. To protect the proceeds of a life insurance policy from an indirect attack by a dependant, one might consider having the policy owned by someone else. For example, a man living in a common-law relationship might have his common-law wife apply for insurance on his life rather than doing so himself. This would protect the proceeds from attack by any of his dependants and would ensure that the monies were paid to the beneficiary designated in the policy.

It is theoretically possible that applications could be brought by a deceased's ex-wife, present wife (from whom he was separated), and common-law wife all at the same time.

These provisions of the *Succession Law Reform Act* must be borne in mind by the personal representative. The distribution of the estate in accordance with a will or in accordance with the intestacy provisions of the *Succession Law Reform Act* could be disturbed by a successful dependant application. Such applications, while not common, are also not rare. If you are involved in the administration of an estate where such an application is brought or may be brought, you must certainly seek legal advice.

5

Steps to Take Prior to Applying for Probate or Administration

1. General

Your first obligation will, of course, be to ascertain whether or not the deceased person had a will. This can often prove difficult, especially in situations where the deceased person had no close relatives familiar with his or her affairs.

As a side note, it is certainly advisable when making a will to give a copy of it to your personal representative and to advise him or her where the original may be found.

However, if this practice has not been followed by the deceased, it may be necessary to conduct a search for the will.

A lawyer who has prepared a will for a client often, at the request of the client, retains the original signed copy of the will in the vault. As well, there is provision in Ontario for a person who has made a will to deposit it for safekeeping in the local office of the Ontario court on payment of a nominal fee, although this is an infrequent practice.

Of course, if the deceased person had a safety deposit box, it is quite likely that the original will can be found in that box. Although it is a general rule that a safety deposit box is frozen at the time of the death of the person in whose name it is maintained, it is possible to gain access to the safety deposit box immediately following the death of the deceased person and, if the will is located there, to remove it from the safety deposit box.

If all else fails, it is possible to place an advertisement in the *Ontario Reports* (reports of judicial decisions circulated to all Ontario lawyers) asking if anyone has any information regarding the deceased's will. It is not uncommon to find these advertisements in the weekly *Ontario Reports*. It is just possible that a lawyer reading the advertisement might be aware of the location of the will or might even have the will in his or her vault.

It is only possible to apply for administration if the applicant is in a position to swear under oath that he or she has made a "careful search and inquiry" for a will of the deceased person.

If such a search is carried out and no will is turned up, an application for Certificate of Appointment of Estate Trustee without a will should be made. Of course, if a will is located, the application will be for a Certificate of Appointment of Estate Trustee with a will.

2. How to Arrange for Burial

Once a will is discovered, it should be reviewed if at all possible before arranging disposition of the remains of the deceased.

It is not uncommon for a person who is making a will to indicate in the will the way in which he or she wishes to be buried. As well, the will may provide for the donation of eyes or other vital organs to medical science (see *Wills for Ontario*, another book in the Self-Counsel series, for advice on how to do this).

It is obvious that arrangements for the burial of the deceased will have to be made before probate or administration can take place.

Funeral directors are generally prepared to wait until after the court grant has been made before demanding payment for their services and, consequently, there should be no need to use the assets of the estate before receiving the appropriate grant from the court.

You will recall that, although executors obtain their power from the will, administrators have no authority whatsoever until the court grants to them a Certificate of Appointment of Estate Trustee without a Will. Therefore, it is very unwise for an applicant to interfere in any way with the assets of the estate before his or her appointment.

Sometimes it is necessary for a family member to incur funeral expenses before probate or administration is complete. In such instances, the person making the expenditure will have a claim against the estate through the personal representative once the appropriate court grant has been made.

3. Who to Notify of the Death

If the deceased person was living alone at the time of death and the post office discovers the fact of the death, mail delivery will be discontinued.

This can be a disadvantage to the personal representative since mail addressed to the deceased is often helpful in locating other assets or debts essential to the probating of the estate.

Accordingly, immediately following death, advise the post office nearest to the home of the deceased and make arrangements for the re-addressing of mail to the address of the personal representative.

As well, all beneficiaries (if there is a will), insurance companies, banks, pension offices, and employers should be notified of the death.

It is necessary to send all persons entitled to a share in the estate a notice of the application for probate or administration (see Sample 9 in Chapter 6 and Sample 17 in Chapter 7). In the case of probate, a copy of the will must be attached to the notice. The notice must be sent to each beneficiary by regular letter mail at the person's last known address. If the beneficiary is younger than the age of 18, the notice must be sent to a parent or guardian of the minor, as well as the Office of the Children's Lawyer. If the beneficiary is mentally incompetent, the notice must be sent to the office of the Public Guardian and Trustee.

If the deceased was collecting old age pension or the Canada Pension at the time of death, the estate is entitled to the payment for the month in which the death occurred, even though the deceased may have died before receiving that payment.

The appropriate department should be advised immediately of the death so that future cheques are not forwarded.

Arrangements should be made to cancel all credit cards and all issuers of such credit cards should be notified of the death as soon as possible and asked to forward their final bills and to close out the accounts.

4. How to Obtain Immediate Cash

If the deceased had a bank account in his or her name, the funds in the account become the property of the estate. If the executor needs money to pay for funeral expenses, probate fees, or other immediate requirements, a meeting should be arranged with the bank manager. The manager will usually be willing to authorize the payment from the account of the estate if he or she is satisfied that the expenses are authentic and that payment cannot be delayed until after the grant of probate.

5. What You Need to Know about the Preparation of an Inventory of Assets

The *Estates Act* requires the total dollar value of the estate. To arrive at such a figure, you must prepare an inventory.

It will be necessary to list all of the assets which the deceased owned at the time of death and to place some valuation on each asset. It may be necessary to have professional appraisals done of items such as jewellery and real estate. If so, such appraisals should be obtained in writing and retained as evidence to back up the valuations placed on these items.

In making this inventory, you should not forget to take into account any life insurance policies, death benefits, or pension benefits that may be payable to the estate of the deceased person.

6. What about the Debts of the Deceased?

A list of the deceased's unpaid debts should also be compiled at this time.

It is, needless to say, necessary to ensure that the assets of the estate are not distributed before all debts are fully paid. Sufficient estate assets should be retained on hand by the personal representative at all times to ensure that all debts can be paid.

As mentioned earlier, you might advertise for creditors. While many lawyers do this as a matter of practice, it is a step that may be omitted in simple estates. (See section 5. of Chapter 2 for a more detailed discussion.)

6

How to Apply for Probate (Certificate of Appointment of Estate Trustee with a Will)

1. Introduction

This chapter deals with the precise step-by-step procedure to be followed in obtaining probate, including the forms that are required to be filed with the court to obtain that grant.

As has been stated, there is no reason why you cannot complete the forms and submit them yourself to the office of the court for processing.

The officials of the court are very helpful and, as mentioned, although they cannot fill in the forms for you (except where the assets of the estate do not exceed $1,000), they will be pleased to give you the advice and information necessary to properly complete them.

2. Documents to Be Submitted to the Court

Sample 3 describes a hypothetical or sample estate that illustrates most of the common problems you will run into when preparing the various forms and documents that must be filed with the court. You should examine the details of the hypothetical estate before trying to understand the forms.

The documentation to be submitted to the court is as follows.

SAMPLE 3
HYPOTHETICAL ESTATE

John Adams Smith died on March 1, 20--, in an automobile accident. John was employed as a truck driver for Gordon Green Transport Ltd. John was only 30. He is survived by a wife, Mary, and three small children: Joanne, Peter, and Gloria. John had a simple will prepared in April 20--, naming Mary as executrix and leaving the bulk of his estate to her. Following is a list of assets which belonged to John at the time of death, including insurance policies payable on account of his death.

(a) House located at 42 Rose Avenue, Toronto, owned jointly with wife, Mary.

(b) A mortgage on 99 Michigan Row, in the Township of Raleigh.

(c) A $20,000 life insurance policy on John with Everyman's Insurance Society of Windsor, payable to the estate.

(d) A $10,000 life insurance policy on John with Canadian Life and Indemnity Corporation, payable to Mary as named beneficiary.

(e) Bank account with United Bank of Canada

(f) Account with Independent Credit Union

(g) Cash in wallet of $77.24

(h) Canada Savings Bonds of $6,000

(i) Intercolonial Pipe Lines Debentures of $10,000

(j) 12 shares of Rainbow Gold Mines Ltd.

(k) 100 shares of Gordon Lumber Inc.

(l) 3 shares of Bell Communications of New Brunswick Limited

(m) 2000 Chevrolet automobile

(n) Household goods and furniture

(o) Miscellaneous jewellery

2.1 Application for Certificate of Appointment of Estate Trustee with a Will

This form (see Sample 4) is the official application submitted to the court outlining information about the deceased, including his or her place of residence, marital status, and date of death. This form must be signed by the executor.

The first section provides details of the deceased, the second section provides details of the value of the estate, and the second page gives details of the applicant or applicants (those named in the will as executor(s)). The second page of the form is actually an affidavit to be sworn under oath by the applicant.

If there is more than one personal representative named in the will, each, individually, must swear the affidavit. Note, too, that details must be provided for each applicant. The affidavit must be signed in the presence of a lawyer, notary, or other commissioner for taking oaths. There is generally a person in the court office in whose presence the affidavit can be sworn. All those signing an affidavit must, however, appear in person before the person taking such affidavit.

In the "value of estate" portion of the form, a total dollar figure for the value of the assets of the estate must be provided as well as a division of this dollar figure between two types of assets: real estate (the net value after taking into account outstanding mortgages) and personal (being all non-real estate assets). No details of the nature of the assets are necessary.

Any property (whether real estate, furniture, stocks and bonds, or a bank account) held by the deceased and any other person jointly does not form part of the estate of the deceased for the purposes of the application to the court.

Under the law of Ontario, any property held jointly passes automatically to the surviving joint owner. Therefore, it does not constitute a part of the estate of the deceased for probate purposes and is, therefore, not included in the "value of estate" portion of the application.

Life insurance payable directly to a named beneficiary falls into the same category. Again, the proceeds of such insurance do not constitute an asset of the estate since they are paid directly to the beneficiary according to the terms of the insurance policy. In cases

SAMPLE 4
APPLICATION FOR CERTIFICATE OF APPOINTMENT OF ESTATE TRUSTEE WITH A WILL

FORM 74.4

Courts of Justice Act

APPLICATION FOR CERTIFICATE OF APPOINTMENT OF ESTATE TRUSTEE
WITH A WILL (INDIVIDUAL APPLICANT)

ONTARIO

SUPERIOR COURT OF JUSTICE

APPLICATION FOR CERTIFICATE OF APPOINTMENT OF ESTATE TRUSTEE WITH A WILL (INDIVIDUAL APPLICANT)
(Form 74.4 Under the Rules)

at   TORONTO
This application is filed by *(insert name and address)*

  MARY MATILDA SMITH, 42 ROSE AVENUE, TORONTO, ONTARIO
DETAILS ABOUT THE DECEASED PERSON

Complete in full as applicable

First given name	Second given name	Third given name	Surname
JOHN	ADAMS		SMITH

And if the deceased was known by any other name(s), state below the full name(s) used including surname.

First given name	Second given name	Third given name	Surname

Date of birth of the deceased person, if known: *(day, month, year)* NOVEMBER 21, 1981

Address of fixed place of abode *(street or postal address) (city or town)*	*(county or district)*
42 ROSE AVENUE	TORONTO

If the deceased person had no fixed place of abode in Ontario, did he or she have property in Ontario? [ ] No [ ] Yes	**Last occupation of deceased person** TRUCK DRIVER

Place of death *(city or town; county or district)*	Date of death *(day, month, year)*	Date of last will (marked as Exhibit "A") *(day, month, year)*
TORONTO, ONTARIO	1 MARCH, 20--	13 APRIL, 20--

Was the deceased person 18 years of age or older at the date of the will (or 21 years of age or older if the will is dated earlier than September 1, 1971)?
If not, explain why certificate is being sought. Give details in an attached schedule.   [   ] No   [X] Yes

Date of codicil (marked as Exhibit "B") *(day, month, year)*	Date of codicil (marked as Exhibit "C") *(day, month, year)*
NONE	NONE

Marital Status   [   ] Unmarried   [X] Married   [   ] Widowed   [   ] Divorced

Did the deceased person marry after the date of the will?
If yes, explain why certificate is being sought. Give details in an attached schedule.   [X] No   [   ] Yes

Was a marriage of the deceased person terminated by a judgment absolute of divorce, or declared a nullity, after the date of the will?
If yes, give details in an attached schedule.   [X] No   [   ] Yes

Is any person who signed the will or a codicil as witness or for the testator, or the spouse of such person a beneficiary under the will?
If yes, give details in an attached schedule.   [X] No   [   ] Yes

RCP-E 74.4 (April 11, 2012)
SELF-COUNSEL PRESS-PROBATE-ONT (FORM 74.4) (1-1)13

VALUE OF ASSETS OF ESTATE

Do not include in the total amount: insurance payable to a named beneficiary or assigned for value, property held jointly and passing by survivorship, or real estate outside Ontario.

Personal property	Real estate, net of encumbrances	Total
$ 58,796.80	$ NIL	$ 58,796.80

Is there any person entitled to an interest in the estate who is not an applicant?   [   ] No   [X] Yes

If a person named in the will or codicil as estate trustee is not an applicant, explain.

If a person not named in the will or a codicil as estate trustee is an applicant, explain why that person is entitled to apply.

If the spouse of the deceased is an applicant, has the spouse elected to receive the entitlement under section 5 of the *Family Law Act*?   [X] No   [   ] Yes
If yes, explain why the spouse is entitled to apply.

AFFIDAVIT(S) OF APPLICANT(S)
(Attach a separate sheet for additional affidavits, if necessary)

I, an applicant named in this application, make oath and say/affirm:

1. I am 18 years of age or older.
2. The exhibit(s) referred to in this application are the last will and each codicil (where applicable) of the deceased person and I do not know of any later will or codicil.
3. I will faithfully administer the deceased person's property according to law and render a complete and true account of my administration when lawfully required.

4. If I am not named as estate trustee in the will or codicil, consents of persons who together have a majority interest in the value of the assets of the estate at the date of death are attached.
5. The information contained in this application and in any attached schedules is true, to the best of my knowledge and belief.

Name *(surname and forename(s))*	Occupation
SMITH, MARY MATILDA	SERVER

Address *(street or postal address)*	*(city or town)*	*(province)*	*(postal code)*
42 ROSE AVENUE	TORONTO	ONTARIO	M9A 2C8

Sworn/Affirmed before me at the CITY

of TORONTO

in the PROVINCE

of ONTARIO   *Mary Matilda Smith*
                                                              Signature of applicant
this 20TH day of MARCH .... , 20 --

_____
A Commissioner for taking Affidavits *(or as may be)*

RCP-E 74.4 (April 11, 2012)
SELF-COUNSEL PRESS-PROBATE-ONT (FORM 74.4) (1-2)13

Name *(surname and forename(s))*	Occupation

Address *(street or postal address)*	*(city or town)*	*(province)*	*(postal code)*

Sworn/Affirmed before me at the ....

of ....

in the ....

of ....

this .... day of ...., 20 ....

_____
A Commissioner for taking Affidavits *(or as may be)*

_____
Signature of applicant

RCP-E 74.4 (April 11, 2012)
SELF-COUNSEL PRESS-PROBATE-ONT (FORM 74.4) (1-3)13

where a life insurance policy is payable to the estate, obviously this does constitute an estate asset and it will be included in the value of the estate filed with the court.

2.2 Affidavit of Execution of Will or Codicil and Affidavit Attesting to the Handwriting and Signature of a Holograph Will

The Affidavit of Execution of Will is the other form that must be filed with the application. This is an affidavit (see Sample 5) made by one of the witnesses to the will (in the case of a will that is not a holograph will) confirming under oath that he or she was present, with the other witness, when the will was signed. (A holograph will is a will wholly in the handwriting of the deceased and signed by him or her. A holograph will needs no witnesses.)

Only one of the two witnesses need sign such an affidavit. If neither of the witnesses is living or if neither can be found, the propriety of the execution of the will can be established in other ways. An affidavit (see Sample 6) would have to be filed with the court to establish that both witnesses are dead, or as the case may be. A further affidavit will be required by someone familiar with the deceased's handwriting, establishing that the signature on the will is that of the person who made the will (see Sample 7).

Sometimes a codicil must also be submitted to the court. A codicil is simply an amendment to a will executed at some date after the original will. The will and the codicil are read together and both must, of course, be submitted to the court with the application. The Affidavit of Execution of Will or Codicil is used in this case. This affidavit is made by one of two witnesses to the codicil or by someone else familiar with the deceased's signature in exactly the same fashion as done for the will.

Many lawyers have adopted the practice of completing the Affidavit of Execution of Will at the same time the will is signed. The advantage of this practice is that the witnesses are readily available to complete the affidavit and will not have to be found at the time of death.

If the will you are seeking to have probated already has an Affidavit of Execution of Will attached to it, you may submit the Affidavit to the court together with the Application for Certificate of Appointment of Estate Trustee.

SAMPLE 5
AFFIDAVIT OF EXECUTION OF WILL OR CODICIL

FORM 74.8

Courts of Justice Act

AFFIDAVIT OF EXECUTION OF WILL OR CODICIL

ONTARIO   *(Court file no.)*

SUPERIOR COURT OF JUSTICE

In the matter of the execution of a will or codicil of JOHN ADAMS SMITH _____ *(insert name)*

AFFIDAVIT

I, JAMES GORDON PETERS _____ ,
       (insert name)

of 1444 LOGAN STREET, CITY OF TORONTO _____ ,
       (insert city or town and county or district, metropolitan or regional municipality of residence)

make oath and say/affirm:

1.   On APRIL 13, 20-- _____ *(date)*, I was present and saw the document marked as Exhibit "A" to this affidavit
executed by JOHN ADAMS SMITH _____ *(insert name)*.

2.   JOHN ADAMS SMITH _____ *(insert name)* executed the document in the presence of myself and
 MARY A. McGRATH, OF THE CITY OF TORONTO *(insert name of other witness and city or town, county or district, metropolitan or
regional municipality of residence)*. We were both present at the same time, and signed the document in the testator's presence as attesting witnesses.

Sworn/Affirmed before me at the CITY ....   )
)
of TORONTO ....   )
)
in the PROVINCE ....   )
)
of ONTARIO ....   )   *James Gordon Peters*
)   _____
this 18TH ......day of MARCH ...., 20 .--   )
)
_____   )
              J.S. Commissioner
A Commissioner for Taking Affidavits *(or as may be)*

NOTE: *If the testator was blind or signed by making his or her mark,
add the following paragraph:*

3. Before its execution, the document was read over to the testator, who
(was blind) (signed by making his or her mark). The testator appeared to
understand the contents.

**WARNING: A beneficiary or the spouse of a beneficiary should not
be a witness.**

RCP-E 74.8 (November 1, 2005)
SELF-COUNSEL PRESS-PROBATE-ONT (FORM 74.8) (3-1)07

A F F I D A V I T

SUPERIOR COURT OF JUSTICE

IN THE ESTATE OF JOHN ADAMS SMITH, DECEASED.

I, KENNETH PETER PIPER, of 1444 Logan Street, in the City of Toronto, in the Municipality of Toronto, make oath and say:

1.   I was a longtime friend of the deceased, John Adams Smith, who resided at 42 Rose Avenue, in the City of Toronto, in the Municipality of Toronto.

2.   I was well acquainted for many years before their deaths with James G. Peters and Mary A. McGrath, the two witnesses to the will of the said John Adams Smith.

3.   Both the said James G. Peters and Mary A. McGrath predeceased the said John Adams Smith. James G. Peters died on or about the 12th day of December, 20--, while Mary A. McGrath died on or about the 4th day of June, 20--. I am aware of both deaths due to my close connection during their lives with both of the said witnesses. I attended the funerals of both James G. Peters and Mary A. McGrath and am certain that both are now dead.

4.   This affidavit is sworn in support of an application by Mary Matilda Smith for the issue of the Certificate of Appointment of Estate Trustee with a Will in the estate of the said John Adams Smith.

SWORN before me in the City of Toronto, in the Province of Ontario, this 8th day of March 20--.	)))))
	Kenneth Piper
	KENNETH PETER PIPER
	)
I. M. Commissioner	)
A Commissioner, etc.	)

A F F I D A V I T

SUPERIOR COURT OF JUSTICE

IN THE ESTATE OF JOHN ADAMS SMITH, DECEASED.

I, WILLIAM CHARLES BELL, of 4 Winlock Crescent, in the Borough of North York, in the Municipality of Toronto, make oath and say:

1. I am employed by Gordon Green Transport Ltd., as chief dispatcher and comptroller. As such I have seen the signature of the deceased John Adams Smith on at least one thousand different occasions on various documents, bills of lading, and receipts.

2. I have examined the signature on the will dated the 13th day of April, 20--, which purports to be the Last Will and Testament of the said John Adams Smith.

3. The signature on the said will is clearly that of the said John Adams Smith. My familiarity with his signature permits me to attest unequivocally to this statement. There is no doubt whatsoever in my mind that the said will was actually signed by the said John Adams Smith.

4. This affidavit is sworn in support of an application by Mary Matilda Smith for the issue of a Certificate of Appointment of Estate Trustee With a Will in the estate of the said John Adams Smith.

SWORN before me in the City of Toronto, in the Province of Ontario, this 18th day of March 20--.	)))) *William C. Bell*) WILLIAM CHARLES BELL))
I. M. Commissioner	)
A Commissioner, etc.	)

Where a holograph will is being probated, proof of validity of the will is not possible through the Affidavit of Execution of Will since there is no witness to sign such affidavit. A different form, the Affidavit Attesting to the Handwriting and Signature of a Holograph Will or Codicil, is filed with the court instead. It is an affidavit of someone familiar with the handwriting and signature of the deceased (see Sample 8).

2.3 Notice of an Application for a Certificate of Appointment and Affidavit of Service of Notice

As explained in Chapter 5, it is necessary to send each person who is entitled to a share of the estate a Notice of an Application for a Certificate of Appointment (see Sample 9), together with a copy of the will. In order to satisfy the court that you have complied with this requirement, you must complete an Affidavit of Service of Notice (see Sample 10). The affidavit is completed by inserting the name of the applicant who served the notice. It is then signed in the presence of a notary or commissioner for taking oaths and filed in court with the other documents that accompany your application.

2.4 The will

The original signed copy of the will (see Sample 11) must be submitted along with the documents outlined above. You will note from the examination of the preceding forms that the will is referred to as an "exhibit" to both the Affidavit of Applicant and the Affidavit of Execution of Will or Codicil.

As well, the last page of the will (the page where the signature of the person who made the will appears) is turned over and, on the back, reference is made to the fact that the will is an exhibit to each of the affidavits.

If there are one or more codicils to the will, the codicil or codicils must also be submitted to the court along with a further Affidavit of Execution of Will or Codicil.

Similar notations to those made on the back of the signing page of the will should also be made on the back of the signing page of the codicil or codicils.

In addition to the original will, you should also provide the court with one photocopy of the will.

SAMPLE 8
AFFIDAVIT ATTESTING TO THE HANDWRITING AND SIGNATURE OF A HOLOGRAPH WILL OR CODICIL

FORM 74.9

Courts of Justice Act

AFFIDAVIT ATTESTING TO THE HANDWRITING AND SIGNATURE OF A HOLOGRAPH WILL OR CODICIL

ONTARIO   *(Court file no.)*

SUPERIOR COURT OF JUSTICE

IN THE ESTATE OF   JOSEPH PETERSON   , deceased.
                                                    (insert name)

AFFIDAVIT ATTESTING TO THE HANDWRITING
AND SIGNATURE OF A HOLOGRAPH WILL OR CODICIL

I, MARIA V.F. SERPA   ,
         (insert name)

of THE CITY OF TORONTO, IN THE MUNICIPALITY OF TORONTO   ,
         (insert city or town and county or district, metropolitan or regional municipality of residence)

make oath and say/affirm:

1.   I was well acquainted with the deceased and have frequently seen the deceased's signature and handwriting.

2.   I believe the whole of the document dated   JANUARY 1, 20--   *(insert date)*, now shown to me and marked as Exhibit "A" to this affidavit, including the signature, is in the handwriting of the deceased.

Sworn/Affirmed before me at the CITY   )
)
of TORONTO   )
)
in the PROVINCE   )
)
of ONTARIO   )   *Maria V.F. Serpa*
)
this 10TH day of JUNE   , 20 --   )
)
_____   )
           J.S. Commissioner
A Commissioner for Taking Affidavits *(or as may be)*

RCP-E 74.9 (November 1, 2005)
SELF-COUNSEL PRESS-PROBATE-ONT (FORM 74.9) (4-1)07

SAMPLE 9
NOTICE OF AN APPLICATION FOR A CERTIFICATE OF APPOINTMENT OF ESTATE TRUSTEE WITH A WILL*

FORM 74.7

Courts of Justice Act

NOTICE OF AN APPLICATION FOR A CERTIFICATE OF APPOINTMENT OF ESTATE TRUSTEE WITH A WILL

ONTARIO   (*Court file no.*)

SUPERIOR COURT OF JUSTICE

IN THE ESTATE OF _____ JOHN ADAMS SMITH _____ , deceased.
                                        (*insert name*)

NOTICE OF AN APPLICATION FOR A
CERTIFICATE OF APPOINTMENT OF ESTATE
TRUSTEE WITH A WILL

1.   The deceased died on MARCH 1, 20-- (*insert date*). The deceased person's date of birth was NOV. 21, 1981 (*insert date, if known*).

2.   Attached to this notice are:

    (A)   If the notice is sent to or in respect of a person entitled only to a specified item of property or stated amount of money, an extract of the part or parts of the will or codicil relating to the gift, or a copy of the will (and codicil(s), if any).

    (B)   If the notice is sent to or in respect of any other beneficiary, a copy of the will (and codicil(s), if any).

    (C)   If the notice is sent to the Children's Lawyer or the Public Guardian and Trustee, a copy of the will (and codicil(s), if any), and if it is not included in the notice, a statement of the estimated value of the interest of the person represented.

3.   The applicant named in this notice is applying for a certificate of appointment of estate trustee with a will.

APPLICANT

Name	Address
MARY MATILDA SMITH	42 ROSE AVENUE, TORONTO, ONTARIO

4.   The following persons who are less than 18 years of age are entitled, whether their interest is contingent or vested, to share in the distribution of the estate:

Name	Date of Birth (*day, month, year*)	Name and Address of Parent or Guardian	Estimated Value of Interest in Estate *
N/A			

*Note: *The Estimated Value of Interest in Estate may be omitted in the form if it is included in a separate schedule attached to the notice sent to the Children's Lawyer.*

5.   The following persons who are mentally incapable within the meaning of section 6 of the *Substitute Decisions Act, 1992* in respect of an issue in the proceeding, and who have guardians or attorneys acting under powers of attorney with authority to act in the proceeding, are entitled, whether their interest is contingent or vested, to share in the distribution of the estate:

Name and Address of Person	Name and Address of Guardian or Attorney *
NONE	

* *Specify whether guardian or attorney.*

RCP-E 74.7 (April 11, 2012)
SELF-COUNSEL PRESS-PROBATE-ONT (FORM 74.7) (2-1)13

*A copy of the above notice must be sent to each person who is entitled to a share of the estate along with a copy of the will. It is not necessary to send the form to the applicant.

6.   The following persons who are mentally incapable within the meaning of section 6 of the *Substitute Decisions Act, 1922* in respect of an issue in the proceeding, and who do not have guardians or attorneys acting under powers of attorney with authority to act in the proceeding, are entitled, whether their interest is contingent or vested, to share in the distribution of the estate:

Name and Address of Person	Estimated Value of Interest in Estate *
NONE	

* **Note:** *The Estimated Value of Interest in Estate may be omitted in the forms if it is included in a separate schedule attached to the notice sent to the Public Guardian and Trustee.*

7.   Unborn or unascertained persons may be entitled to share in the distribution of the estate. *(Delete if not applicable.)*

8.   All other persons and charities entitled, whether their interest is contingent or vested, to share in the distribution of the estate are as follows:

Name	Address
MARY MATILDA SMITH	42 ROSE AVENUE, TORONTO, ONTARIO
EDWARD SMITH	42 FIRST STREET, TORONTO, ONTARIO

9.   This notice is being sent, by regular lettermail, to all adult persons and charities named above in this notice (except to an applicant who is entitled to share in the distribution of the estate), to the Public Guardian and Trustee if paragraph 6 applies, to a parent or guardian of the minor and to the Children's Lawyer if paragraph 4 applies, to the guardian or attorney if paragraph 5 applies, and to the Children's Lawyer if paragraph 7 applies.

10.   The following persons named in the Will or being a member of a class of beneficiaries under the Will may be entitled to be served but have not been served for the reasons shown below:

Name of person (as it appears in will, if applicable)	Reason not served
NOT APPLICABLE	

If paragraph 10 does not apply, insert "Not applicable."

DATE: MARCH 18, 20--

RCP-E 74.7 (April 11, 2012)
SELF-COUNSEL PRESS-PROBATE-ONT (FORM 74.7) (2-2)13

SAMPLE 10
AFFIDAVIT OF SERVICE OF NOTICE (WITH A WILL)

FORM 74.6

Courts of Justice Act

AFFIDAVIT OF SERVICE OF NOTICE

ONTARIO   *(Court file no.)*

SUPERIOR COURT OF JUSTICE

IN THE ESTATE OF   JOHN ADAMS SMITH   , deceased.
                                                (insert name)

AFFIDAVIT OF SERVICE OF NOTICE

I, MARY MATILDA SMITH   ,
       (insert name)

of THE CITY OF TORONTO   ,
       (insert city or town and county or district, metropolitan or regional municipality of residence)

make oath and say/affirm:

1.   I am an applicant for a certificate of appointment of estate trustee with a will in the estate.

2.   I have sent or caused to be sent a notice in Form 74.7, a copy of which is marked as Exhibit "A" to this affidavit, to all adult persons and charities named in the notice (except to an applicant who is entitled to share in the distribution of the estate), to the Public Guardian and Trustee if paragraph 6 of the notice applies, to a parent or guardian of the minor and to the Children's Lawyer if paragraph 4 applies, to the guardian or attorney if paragraph 5 applies, and to the Children's Lawyer if paragraph 7 applies, all by regular lettermail sent to the person's last known address.

3.   I have attached or caused to be attached to each notice the following:

   (A)   In the case of a notice sent to or in respect of a person entitled only to a specified item of property or stated amount of money, an extract of the part or parts of the will or codicil relating to the gift, or a copy of the will (and codicil(s), if any).

   (B)   In the case of a notice sent to or in respect of any other beneficiary, a copy of the will (and codicil(s), if any).

   (C)   In the case of a notice sent to the Children's Lawyer or the Public Guardian and Trustee, a copy of the will (and codicil(s), if any) and a statement of the estimated value of the interest of the person represented.

4.   The following persons and charities specifically named in the Will are not entitled to be served for the reasons shown:

   Name of person (as it appears in will, if applicable)   **Reason not served**

   NOT APPLICABLE

   If paragraph 4 does not apply insert "Not Applicable."

5.   The following persons named in the Will or being a member of a class of beneficiaries under the Will may be entitled to be served but have not been served for the reasons shown below:

   Name of person (as it appears in will, if applicable)   **Reason not served**

   NOT APPLICABLE

   If paragraph 5 does not apply insert "Not Applicable."

RCP-E 74.6 (November 1, 2005)
SELF-COUNSEL PRESS-PROBATE-ONT (FORM 74.6) (5-1)07

SAMPLE 10 — CONTINUED

6.   To the best of my knowledge and belief, subject to paragraph 5 (if applicable), the persons named in the notice are all the persons who are entitled to share in the distribution of the estate.

Sworn/Affirmed before me at the CITY ....)
)
of TORONTO ....)
)
in the PROVINCE ....)
)
of ONTARIO ....)   _____
)   *Mary Matilda Smith*
this 23RD day of FEBRUARY .... , 20 --)   Signature of applicant
)
_____)

A Commissioner for taking Affidavits *(or as may be)*

RCP-E 74.6 (November 1, 2005)
SELF-COUNSEL PRESS-PROBATE-ONT (FORM 74.6) (5-2)07

THIS IS THE LAST WILL AND TESTAMENT of me, JOHN ADAMS SMITH, of the City of Toronto, in the Province of Ontario, Truck Driver.

1. I HEREBY REVOKE all wills, codicils and testamentary dispositions of every nature and kind whatsoever by me heretofore made.

2. I NOMINATE, CONSTITUTE AND APPOINT my wife, MARY MATILDA SMITH, to be the executrix and trustee of this my will.

3. I GIVE, DEVISE AND BEQUEATH my gold watch to my brother, EDWARD SMITH, for his own use absolutely.

4. I GIVE, DEVISE AND BEQUEATH all the rest and residue of my property of every nature and kind and wheresoever situate, including any property over which I may have a general power of appointment, to my said wife, MARY MATILDA SMITH, for her own use absolutely.

IN TESTIMONY WHEREOF I have to this my last will and testament written upon this single page of paper subscribed my name this 13th day of April, 20--.

SIGNED, PUBLISHED AND DECLARED)
by the said Testator, JOHN ADAMS)
SMITH, as and for his last will and)
testament, in the presence of us,)
both present at the same time, who,)   *John Adam Smith*
at his request in his presence and)   JOHN ADAMS SMITH
in the presence of each other have)
hereunto subscribed our names as)
witnesses.

Witness: _I. M. Witness_   Witness: _I.C. Ewe_
Address: 1013 Main Street,   Address: 81 James St.
Toronto   Toronto
Occupation: Solicitor   Occupation: Secretary

This is Exhibit "A" to the affidavit of Mary Matilda Smith sworn before me this 18th day of March, 20--.

                            I. M. Commissioner
                            A Commissioner, etc.

This is Exhibit "A" to the affidavit of James G. Peters sworn before me this 18th day of March, 20--.

                            I. M. Commissioner
                            A Commissioner, etc.

2.5 Affidavit of Condition of Will

While the above-mentioned documents constitute those normally required to be submitted to the court to obtain a Certificate of Appointment, an additional form will be required in some circumstances. This happens when there are changes, deletions, or additions made which appear in the body of the will or in a codicil to a will.

This additional document is known as the Affidavit of Condition of Will or Codicil and is completed by one of the witnesses to the will or by some person having knowledge of the facts (see Sample 12).

It recites in detail any changes, additions, or interlineations which appear in the will or codicil and must recite whether these changes were made before or after the will was signed.

As is the case with all affidavits, the Affidavit of Condition of Will must be sworn before a lawyer, notary public, or a commissioner for taking oaths.

2.6 Certificate of Appointment of Estate Trustee with a Will

This document must be completed by inserting the name, address, occupation, and date of death of the deceased, and the name, address, and occupation of the applicant (see Sample 13). It is then presented to the court office with the other documents. If the application is approved, it is returned to you with the signature of the registrar and the seal of the court.

2.7 Renunciation

As mentioned in Chapter 2, an executor is not obliged to accept his or her appointment and may renounce by signing a Renunciation of Right to a Certificate of Appointment of Estate Trustee with a Will (see Sample 14). If there are two or more executors named in the will and the other executor(s) wish to accept the appointment, the renunciation must be signed by the executor who does not wish to act and filed together with the Application for a Certificate of Appointment.

2.8 Consent to Applicant's Appointment as Estate Trustee with a Will

Occasionally a situation will arise where there is a valid will but there is no executor available. This may happen because the executor named in the will is mentally infirm or deceased, or does not wish

SAMPLE 12
AFFIDAVIT OF CONDITION OF WILL OR CODICIL

FORM 74.10

Courts of Justice Act

AFFIDAVIT OF CONDITION OF WILL OR CODICIL

ONTARIO

(Court file no.)

SUPERIOR COURT OF JUSTICE

IN THE ESTATE OF   JOHN ADAMS SMITH   , deceased.
         (insert name)

AFFIDAVIT OF CONDITION OF WILL OR CODICIL

I,   JAMES GORDON PETERS   ,
     (insert name)

of   THE CITY OF TORONTO   ,
    (insert city or town and county or district, metropolitan or regional municipality of residence)

make oath and say/affirm:

1.   On   APRIL 13, 20--   *(date)*, I was present and saw the document marked as Exhibit "A" to this affidavit executed by the deceased, in the presence of myself and   MARY A. McGRATH   *(insert name of other witness)*.

2.   The following alterations, erasures, obliterations or interlineations that have not been attested appear in the document:

     NONE

3.   The document is now in the same condition as when it was executed.

Sworn/Affirmed before me at the CITY)	
of TORONTO)	
in the PROVINCE)	
of ONTARIO)	*James Gordon Peters*
this 15TH day of JULY , 20 --)	
I.B. Commissioner)	

A Commissioner for taking Affidavits *(or as may be)*

NOTE: *If paragraph 3 is not correct, add the words "except that" and give details of the exceptions.*

RCP-E 74.10 (November 1, 2005)
SELF-COUNSEL PRESS-PROBATE-ONT (FORM 74.10) (6-1)07

SAMPLE 13
CERTIFICATE OF APPOINTMENT OF ESTATE TRUSTEE WITH A WILL

FORM 74.13

Courts of Justice Act

CERTIFICATE OF APPOINTMENT OF ESTATE TRUSTEE WITH A WILL

ONTARIO   *(Court file no.)*

SUPERIOR COURT OF JUSTICE

IN THE ESTATE OF JOHN ADAMS SMITH   *(insert name)*, deceased,

late of THE CITY OF TORONTO, ONTARIO

occupation TRUCK DRIVER

who died on MARCH 1, 20--

CERTIFICATE OF APPOINTMENT OF ESTATE TRUSTEE WITH A WILL

Applicant	Address	Occupation
MARY MATILDA SMITH	42 ROSE AVENUE, TORONTO, ONTARTIO	SERVER

This CERTIFICATE OF APPOINTMENT OF ESTATE TRUSTEE WITH A WILL is hereby issued under the seal of the court to the applicant named above. A copy of the deceased's last will (and codicil(s), if any) is attached.

DATE

Registrar
Address of court office
330 UNIVERSITY AVENUE, 7TH FLOOR
TORONTO, ONTARIO
M5G 1R7

RCP-E 74.13 (November 1, 2005)
SELF-COUNSEL PRESS-PROBATE-ONT (FORM 74.13) (10-1)07

Court file no.

ONTARIO
SUPERIOR COURT OF JUSTICE

at

IN THE ESTATE OF

JOHN ADAMS SMITH   , deceased.

**CERTIFICATE OF
APPOINTMENT
OF ESTATE TRUSTEE
WITH A WILL**
(Form 74.13 under the Rules)
JANUARY 1995

*Name, address, telephone number and fax number of
solicitor or applicant:*

MARY MATILDA SMITH
42 ROSE AVENUE,
TORONTO, ONTARIO

SAMPLE 14
RENUNCIATION OF RIGHT TO A CERTIFICATE OF APPOINTMENT
OF ESTATE TRUSTEE WITH A WILL

FORM 74.11

Courts of Justice Act

RENUNCIATION OF RIGHT TO A CERTIFICATE OF APPOINTMENT OF ESTATE TRUSTEE
(OR SUCCEEDING ESTATE TRUSTEE) WITH A WILL

ONTARIO   *(Court file no.)*

SUPERIOR COURT OF JUSTICE

IN THE ESTATE OF   JOHN EDWARD JONES   , deceased.
                                        (insert name)

RENUNCIATION OF RIGHT TO A CERTIFICATE OF APPOINTMENT OF ESTATE TRUSTEE
(OR SUCCEEDING ESTATE TRUSTEE) WITH A WILL

The deceased died on _____ JANUARY 20, 20-- _____ *(date)*.

In that person's testamentary document dated _____ NOVEMBER 15, 20-- _____ *(date)*, I, _____ JENNIFER JONES _____
(insert name), was named an estate trustee.

I renounce my right to a certificate of appointment of estate trustee (or succeeding estate trustee) with a will.

DATE   FEBRUARY 23, 20--

```
                                              )
                                              )
                                              )
                                              )
......I.M. Witness..............              )      ......Jennifer Jones..............
Signature of witness                          )      Signature of person renouncing
                                              )
                                              )
                                              )
```

RCP-E 74.11 (November 1, 2005)
SELF-COUNSEL PRESS-PROBATE-ONT (FORM 74.11) (7-1)07

to act as executor and has renounced, or simply because the will does not name an executor. In each of these cases, any interested person may apply to the court for a Certificate of Appointment as Estate Trustee with a Will (see Sample 13).

Because the applicant is not named in the will as an executor, the consent to his or her appointment must be obtained from the beneficiaries of the estate (see Sample 15). If the consent of all of the beneficiaries cannot be easily obtained, it is sufficient to obtain consent from the beneficiaries who together have a majority interest in the assets of the estate.

2.9 Security

An applicant described in section **2.8** above, as well as an applicant who does not reside in Canada, may be required to post security with the court similar to the security requirements when there is no will at all. A detailed discussion of the requirements for security may be found in Chapter 3.

3. Filing Procedure and Court Fees

Once the various documents have been properly signed and sworn (where necessary), one signed copy of each, along with the will and any codicils, is delivered to the office of the court for the particular county. Chapter 1 discusses the proper court for filing the application.

These documents will generally be reviewed at the time of submission to make sure that they are in order. A tax is payable to the court at the rate of $5 for every $1,000 of estate assets up to $50,000, and $15 for every $1,000 of assets over $50,000. This tax can be paid at the time of submitting the application or you can await an invoice from the court after the documents have received final approval. Also, a fee may be required depending on the type of document sworn.

In order to speed up the process, however, it is advisable to pay the appropriate tax at the time of submitting the documentation. Payment must be by cash or certified cheque, made payable to the "Minister of Finance."

In such circumstances, the Certificate of Appointment will be forwarded to you once it has been issued by the court (see Sample 13). Allow approximately three weeks in the busier centres for the papers to be processed.

SAMPLE 15
CONSENT TO APPLICANT'S APPOINTMENT AS ESTATE TRUSTEE
WITH A WILL

FORM 74.12

Courts of Justice Act

CONSENT TO APPLICANT'S APPOINTMENT AS ESTATE TRUSTEE WITH A WILL

ONTARIO   *(Court file no.)*

SUPERIOR COURT OF JUSTICE

IN THE ESTATE OF   JOHN EDWARD JONES   , deceased.
                                         (insert name)

CONSENT TO APPLICANT'S APPOINTMENT AS ESTATE TRUSTEE WITH A WILL

The deceased died on _JANUARY 20, 20--_ *(date)*.

No estate trustee named in a testamentary document of that person is applying for a certificate of appointment of estate trustee with a will.

I, _JENNIFER JONES_ *(insert name)*, am entitled to share in the distribution of the estate.

I consent to the application by _GLORIA JONES_ *(insert name)* for a certificate of appointment of estate trustee with a will.

I consent to an order dispensing with the filing of a bond by the applicant *(delete if inapplicable)*.

DATE FEBRUARY 23, 20--

.... *Gloria Jones* ....   )   .... *Jennifer Jones* ....
Signature of witness   )   Signature of person consenting
)
)
)
)
)
)

RCP-E 74.12 (November 1, 2005)
SELF-COUNSEL PRESS-PROBATE-ONT (FORM 74.12) (8-1)07

4. Summary of Process

To summarize, you need the following documents with you when you visit the court:

(a) Application for Certificate of Appointment as Estate Trustee (Sample 4)

(b) Affidavit of Execution of Will (where the will has two witnesses) (Sample 5)

(c) Affidavit Confirming Death of Witness (Sample 6) and Affidavit Confirming Signature of Deceased (Sample 7) (if neither witness is living or cannot be found)

(d) Affidavit Attesting to the Handwriting and Signature of a Holograph Will (where the will is a holograph will) (Sample 8)

(e) Original and one photocopy of will and codicils (if any)

(f) Affidavit of Service of Notice (Sample 10) (Notice of an Application for Certificate of Appointment as Estate Trustee, along with a copy of the will, must be sent to each person who is entitled to a share of the estate)

(g) Affidavit of Condition of Will (if required; check with court first) (Sample 12)

(h) Certificate of Appointment of Estate Trustee with a Will (Sample 13)

(i) Renunciation (if required) (Sample 14)

(j) Consent to Applicant's Appointment as Estate Trustee (if required) (Sample 15)

(k) Security (if required)

7

How To Apply for Administration (Certificate of Appointment of Estate Trustee without a Will)

1. General

In the last chapter we dealt with the forms and procedure for applying to the court for a Certificate of Appointment of Estate Trustee with a Will. As discussed in previous chapters, if the deceased person died intestate (i.e., without a will) the appropriate application is for the issuance of a Certificate of Appointment of Estate Trustee without a Will.

2. Applying for a Certificate of Appointment of Estate Trustee without a Will

When applying for a Certificate of Appointment of Estate Trustee without a Will, the procedure is basically the same as the procedure followed when there is a will.

Again, no personal appearance before a judge is necessary. It is simply a matter of filing various documents with the Superior Court of the county or district in which the deceased resided at the time of his or her death.

2.1 Application for Certificate of Appointment of Estate Trustee without a Will

This form is very similar to the form that was discussed in the previous chapter. It sets out details about the deceased person and the value of the estate.

The main difference is that the form contains a statement made under oath by the applicant that he or she has made a careful search and inquiry for a will and that he or she believes no will was left by the deceased. As well, the application sets forth the various heirs and next-of-kin of the deceased who will inherit the estate (see Sample 16).

If the deceased or his or her spouse had ever been divorced it is necessary to attach a schedule to the application, setting out the particulars of the divorce.

2.2 Affidavit of Service of Notice

This is the same form described in Chapter 6 (Sample 10), except that it refers to your Application for Certificate of Appointment of Estate Trustee without a Will (see Sample 16). As explained in Chapter 5, it is necessary to send a notice of your application to all persons who are entitled to share in the distribution of the estate (see Sample 17). Since there is no will, it obviously is not attached to the notice, and it is not mentioned in the Affidavit of Service of Notice. The Affidavit of Service of Notice is signed in the presence of a notary public and filed with the other documents (see Sample 18).

2.3 Renunciation and Consent

In Chapter 3 the persons entitled to apply for a Certificate of Appointment of Estate Trustee without a Will were described.

Sometimes a person with the superior or equal right to apply chooses not to do so and prefers to allow another individual to become the estate trustee. An example of this would be the son of the deceased applying when the deceased had been survived by a widow and two sons. In that situation, two forms known as Renunciation of Prior Right to a Certificate of Appointment of Estate Trustee without a Will (see Sample 19) and Consent to Applicant's Appointment as Estate Trustee without a Will (see Sample 20) must be completed by both the widow and the other son in order to complete the application.

2.4 Administration Bond

Chapter 3 discussed the concept of the bond required in an Application for Certificate of Appointment of Estate Trustee without a Will, unless a court order is obtained dispensing with it.

If you need to post a bond, you should consult with a bonding company, which will provide you with all the information and forms you will need.

Where the following requirements are satisfied, no bond is required, nor is any application needed to dispense with it:

(a) You are the widow or widower applying for administration of your spouse's estate.

(b) The net assets of the estate do not exceed $200,000.

(c) There are no debts to pay (mortgage payments excluded).

If such circumstances exist, an affidavit setting forth the facts (see Sample 21) is filed with the Application for Certificate of Appointment.

2.5 Certificate of Appointment of Estate Trustee without a Will

This document must be completed by inserting the name, address, occupation, and date of death of the deceased, and the name, address, and occupation of the applicant (see Sample 22). It is then presented to the court with the other documents. If the applicant is approved, it is returned to you with the signature of the registrar and the seal of the court.

Once the application has been completed, the procedure for making application is identical to that for applying with a will. The documents are simply filed at the local office of the Ontario Court (General Division).

The same tax structure applies, the applicant paying $5 for every $1,000 worth of estate assets under $50,000 and $15 for every $1,000 worth of estate assets over $50,000.

3. Summary of Process

To summarize, you need the following documents with you when you visit the court:

(a) Application for Certificate of Appointment of Estate Trustee without a Will (Sample 16)

(b) Affidavit of Service of Notice (Sample 18) (Notice of an Application for a Certificate of Appointment of Estate Trustee without a Will must be sent to each person who is entitled to a share of the estate.)

(c) Renunciation (if required) (Sample 19)

(d) Consent to Applicant's Appointment as Estate Trustee without a Will (if required) (Sample 20)

(e) Security (if required)

(f) Certificate of Appointment of Estate Trustee without a Will (Sample 22)

SAMPLE 16
APPLICATION FOR CERTIFICATE OF APPOINTMENT OF ESTATE TRUSTEE WITHOUT A WILL

FORM 74.14

Courts of Justice Act

APPLICATION FOR CERTIFICATE OF APPOINTMENT OF ESTATE TRUSTEE
WITHOUT A WILL (INDIVIDUAL APPLICANT)

ONTARIO

SUPERIOR COURT OF JUSTICE

**APPLICATION FOR CERTIFICATE
OF APPOINTMENT OF ESTATE TRUSTEE
WITHOUT A WILL
(INDIVIDUAL APPLICANT)**
(Form 74.14 Under the Rules)

at TORONTO

This application is filed by *(insert name and address)*

WILLIAM REID, 517 BLACK AVENUE, TORONTO, ONTARIO

DETAILS ABOUT THE DECEASED PERSON

Complete in full as applicable

First given name	Second given name	Third given name	Surname
FRANK			REID

And if the deceased was known by any other name(s), state below the full name(s) used including surname.

First given name	Second given name	Third given name	Surname

Date of birth of the deceased person, if known: *(day, month, year)* NOVEMBER 21, 1981

Address of fixed place of abode *(street or postal address) (city or town)*	*(county or district)*
2300 BLUE AVENUE, TORONTO, ONTARIO	ONTARIO

If the deceased person had no fixed place of abode in Ontario, did he or she have property in Ontario? [ ] No [ ] Yes	**Last occupation of deceased person** CLERK

Place of death *(city or town; county or district)*	**Date of death** *(day, month, year)*
CITY OF TORONTO	4 JUNE 20--

Marital Status	[ ] Unmarried	[X] Married	[ ] Widowed	[ ] Divorced

Was the deceased person's marriage terminated by a judgment absolute of divorce, or declared a nullity? If yes, give details in an attached schedule.	[X] No [ ] Yes
Did the deceased person go through a form of marriage with a person where it appears uncertain whether an earlier marriage of the deceased person had been terminated by divorce or declared a nullity? If yes, give the other person's name and address, and the names and addresses of any children (including deceased children) of the marriage, in an attached schedule.	[X] No [ ] Yes
Was any earlier marriage of a person with whom the deceased person went through a form of marriage terminated by divorce or declared a nullity? If yes, give details in an attached schedule.	[X] No [ ] Yes
Was the deceased person immediately before his or her death living with a person in a conjugal relationship outside marriage? If yes, give the person's name and address in an attached schedule.	[X] No [ ] Yes

RCP-E 74.14 (April 11, 2012)
SELF-COUNSEL PRESS-PROBATE-ONT (FORM 74.14) (11-1)13

SAMPLE 16 — CONTINUED

PERSONS ENTITLED TO SHARE IN THE ESTATE

(Attach a schedule if more space is needed. If a person entitled to share in the estate is not a spouse, child, parent, brother or sister of the deceased person, show how the relationship is traced.)

Name	Address	Relationship to deceased person	Age (if under 18)
JEAN REID	2300 BLUE AVENUE, TORONTO, ONTARIO	SPOUSE	
WILLIAM REID	517 BLACK AVENUE, TORONTO, ONTARIO	SON	

VALUE OF ASSETS OF ESTATE

Do not include in the total amount: insurance payable to a named beneficiary or assigned for value, property held jointly and passing by survivorship, or real estate outside Ontario.

Personal property	Real estate, net of encumbrances	Total
$ 15,000.00	$ NIL	$ 15,000.00

Explain why the applicant is entitled to apply.

SON OF DECEASED AND NOMINEE OF NEXT-OF-KIN.

AFFIDAVIT(S) OF APPLICANT(S)
(Attach a separate sheet for additional affidavits, if necessary)

I, an applicant named in this application, make oath and say/affirm:

1. I am 18 years of age or older and a resident of Ontario.
2. I have made a careful search and inquiry for a will or other testamentary document of the deceased person, but none has been found. I believe that the person did not leave a will or other testamentary document.
3. I will faithfully administer the deceased person's property according to law and render a complete and true account of my administration when lawfully required.
4. Consents of persons who together have a majority interest in the value of the assets of the estate at the date of death are attached.
5. The information contained in this application and in any attached schedules is true, to the best of my knowledge and belief.

Name *(surname and forename(s))*	Occupation
REID, WILLIAM	TEACHER

Address *(street or postal address)*	*(city or town)*	*(province)*	*(postal code)*
517 BLACK AVENUE	TORONTO	ONTARIO	Z1P 0G0

Sworn/Affirmed before me at the CITY)
of TORONTO)
in the PROVINCE)
of ONTARIO)
this 23RD day of AUGUST , 20 --)
)

William Reid
Signature of applicant

A Commissioner for taking Affidavits *(or as may be)*

RCP-E 74.14 (April 11, 2012)
SELF-COUNSEL PRESS-PROBATE-ONT (FORM 74.14) (11-2)13

SAMPLE 16 — CONTINUED

Name *(surname and forename(s))*	Occupation

Address *(street or postal address)*   *(city or town)*   *(province)*   *(postal code)*

Sworn/Affirmed before me at the ....)
)
of ....)
)
in the ....)
)
of ....)
) _____
this .... day of ...., 20 ....)   Signature of applicant
)
_____)
A Commissioner for taking Affidavits *(or as may be)*

RCP-E 74.14 (April 11, 2012)
SELF-COUNSEL PRESS—PROBATE-ONT (FORM 74.14) (11-5)13

SAMPLE 17
NOTICE OF APPLICATION FOR A CERTIFICATE OF APPOINTMENT OF ESTATE TRUSTEE WITHOUT A WILL

FORM 74.17

Courts of Justice Act

NOTICE OF AN APPLICATION FOR A
CERTIFICATE OF APPOINTMENT OF ESTATE TRUSTEE WITHOUT A WILL

ONTARIO   *(Court file no.)*

SUPERIOR COURT OF JUSTICE

IN THE ESTATE OF   _____FRANK REID_____   , deceased.
                                           (insert name)

NOTICE OF AN APPLICATION FOR A
CERTIFICATE OF APPOINTMENT OF ESTATE TRUSTEE WITHOUT A WILL

1.   The deceased died on _JUNE 4, 20--_____ *(insert date)*, without a will.

2.   The applicant named in this notice is applying for a certificate of appointment of estate trustee without a will.

APPLICANT

Name	Address
WILLIAM REID	517 BLACK AVENUE, TORONTO, ONTARIO

3.   The following persons who are less than 18 years of age are entitled to share in the distribution of the estate:

Name	Date of Birth *(day, month, year)*	Name and Address of Parent or Guardian	Estimated Value of Interest in Estate
NONE			

* Note: *The Estimated Value of Interest in Estate may be omitted in the form if it is included in a separate schedule attached to the notice sent to the Children's Lawyer.*

4.   The following persons who are mentally incapable within the meaning of section 6 of the *Substitute Decisions Act, 1992* in respect of an issue in the proceeding, and who have guardians or attorneys acting under powers of attorney with authority to act in the proceeding, are entitled to share in the distribution of the estate:

Name and Address of Person	Name and Address of Guardian or Attorney *
NONE	

* *Specify whether guardian or attorney.*

5.   The following persons who are mentally incapable within the meaning of section 6 of the *Substitute Decisions Act, 1992* in respect of an issue in the proceeding, and who do not have guardians or attorneys acting under powers of attorney with authority to act in the proceeding, are entitled to share in the distribution of the estate:

Name and Address of Person	Estimated Value of Interest in Estate
NONE	

* Note: *The Estimated Value of Interest in Estate may be omitted in the form if it is included in a separate schedule attached to the notice sent to the Public Guardian and Trustee.*

RCP-E 74.17 (November 1, 2005)
SELF-COUNSEL PRESS-PROBATE-ONT (FORM 74.17) (12-1)07

6. All other persons entitled to share in the distribution of the estate are as follows:

Name	Address
JEAN REID	2300 BLUE AVENUE, TORONTO, ONTARIO
WILLIAM REID	517 BLACK AVENUE, TORONTO, ONTARIO

7. This notice is being sent, by regular lettermail, to all adult persons named above in this notice (except to an applicant who is entitled to share in the distribution of the estate), to a parent or guardian of the minor and to the Children's Lawyer if paragraph 3 applies, to the guardian or attorney if paragraph 4 applies, and to the Public Guardian and Trustee if paragraph 5 applies.

8. The following persons may be entitled to be served but have not been served for the reasons shown below:

Name of person	Reason not served
NOT APPLICABLE	

If paragraph 8 does not apply, insert "Not Applicable."

DATE AUGUST 15, 20--

RCP-E 74.17 (November 1, 2005)
SELF-COUNSEL PRESS-PROBATE-ONT (FORM 74.17) (12-2)07

SAMPLE 18
AFFIDAVIT OF SERVICE OF NOTICE (WITHOUT A WILL)

FORM 74.16

Courts of Justice Act

AFFIDAVIT OF SERVICE OF NOTICE

ONTARIO   *(Court file no.)*

SUPERIOR COURT OF JUSTICE

IN THE ESTATE OF   _____ FRANK REID _____   , deceased.
                                               (insert name)

AFFIDAVIT OF SERVICE OF NOTICE

I,   WILLIAM REID _____ ,
       (insert name)

of   THE CITY OF TORONTO _____ ,
    (insert city or town and county or district, metropolitan or regional municipality of residence)

make oath and say/affirm:

1.   I am an applicant for a certificate of appointment of estate trustee without a will in the estate.

2.   I have sent or caused to be sent a notice in Form 74.17, a copy of which is marked as Exhibit "A" to this affidavit, to all adult persons named in the notice (except to an applicant who is entitled to share in the distribution of the estate), to a parent or guardian of the minor and to the Children's Lawyer if paragraph 3 of the notice applies, to the guardian or attorney if paragraph 4 applies and to the Public Guardian and Trustee if paragraph 5 applies, all by regular lettermail sent to the person's last known address.

3.   The following persons may be entitled to be served but have not been served for the reasons shown below:

      Name of person (if applicable)   **Reason not served**

      NOT APPLICABLE

      If paragraph 3 does not apply, insert "Not Applicable."

4.   To the best of my knowledge and belief, subject to paragraph 3 (if applicable), the persons named in the notice are all the persons who are entitled to share in the distribution of the estate.

Sworn/Affirmed before me at the   CITY ....   )
)
of   TORONTO ....   )
)
in the   PROVINCE ....   )
)
of   ONTARIO ....   )   _____
)   *William Reid*
this   15TH   day of   AUGUST .... , 20 --   )
)
_____   )
           I.B. Commissioner
A Commissioner for Taking Affidavits *(or as may be)*

RCP-E 74.16 (November 1, 2005)
SELF-COUNSEL PRESS-PROBATE-ONT (FORM 74.16) (13-1)07

SAMPLE 19
RENUNCIATION OF PRIOR RIGHT TO A CERTIFICATE OF APPOINTMENT OF ESTATE TRUSTEE WITHOUT A WILL

FORM 74.18

Courts of Justice Act

RENUNCIATION OF PRIOR RIGHT TO A CERTIFICATE OF
APPOINTMENT OF ESTATE TRUSTEE WITHOUT A WILL

ONTARIO   *(Court file no.)*

SUPERIOR COURT OF JUSTICE

IN THE ESTATE OF _____ FRANK REID _____ , deceased.
                                 (insert name)

**RENUNCIATION OF PRIOR RIGHT TO A CERTIFICATE OF
APPOINTMENT OF ESTATE TRUSTEE WITHOUT A WILL**

The deceased died on _JUNE 4, 20--_____ *(date)*, without a will.

I, _JEAN REID_____*(insert name)*, am entitled to apply for a certificate of appointment of estate trustee
without a will in priority to _WILLIAM REID_____ *(insert name)*.

I renounce my right to a certificate of appointment of estate trustee without a will in priority to _WILLIAM REID_____
(insert name).

DATE JUNE 20, 20--

	)	
	)	
	)	
	)	
I.M. Witness	)	*Jean Read*
Signature of witness	)	Signature of person renouncing
	)	
	)	
	)	

RCP-E 74.18 (November 1, 2005)
SELF-COUNSEL PRESS-PROBATE-ONT (FORM 74.18) (17-1)07

SAMPLE 20
CONSENT TO APPLICANT'S APPOINTMENT AS ESTATE TRUSTEE WITHOUT A WILL

FORM 74.19

Courts of Justice Act

CONSENT TO APPLICANT'S APPOINTMENT AS ESTATE TRUSTEE WITHOUT A WILL

ONTARIO

(Court file no.)

SUPERIOR COURT OF JUSTICE

IN THE ESTATE OF   FRANK REID   , deceased.
(insert name)

CONSENT TO APPLICANT'S APPOINTMENT AS ESTATE TRUSTEE WITHOUT A WILL

The deceased died on _JUNE 4, 20--_ (date), without a will.

I, _JEAN REID_ (insert name), am entitled to share in the distribution of the estate.

I consent to the application by _WILLIAM REID_ (insert name) for a certificate of appointment of estate trustee without a will.

I consent to an order dispensing with the filing of a bond by the applicant (*delete if inapplicable*).

DATE JUNE 20, 20--

)
)
)
)
)
)
)
)

........I.M. Witness........
Signature of witness

........*Jean Reid*........
Signature of person consenting

RCP-E 74.19 (November 1, 2005)
SELF-COUNSEL PRESS-PROBATE-ONT (FORM 74.19) (18-1)07

IN THE SUPERIOR COURT OF JUSTICE

IN THE ESTATE OF FRANK REID, Retired, Deceased.

AFFIDAVIT RE DEBTS

I, JEAN REID, of 77 Lawrence Avenue West, Apt. 307, in the Borough of North York in the Municipality of Toronto, Widow, make oath and say as follows:

1.   I am the applicant for a Certificate of Appointment of Estate Trustee in connection with the above-noted estate.

2.   As the widow of the deceased, Frank Reid, I am fully familiar with the affairs of my late husband, having handled the financial affairs of our family for several years prior to my husband's death.

3.   All of the debts of the estate have been fully paid, there being no outstanding amounts owing. Having handled all matters relating to the estate to this point, I am fully familiar with the matters herein set out.

4.   I hereby request dispensation with the bond normally required under the provisions of the *Estates Act*, due to the fact that the net value of the estate as computed for the purposes of Section 46 of the *Succession Law Reform Act* does not exceed $200,000.

SWORN before me in the City of Toronto, in the Province of Ontario, this 20th day of June 20--.	)))) *Jean Reid*) JEAN REID)
I. M. Commissioner A Commissioner, etc.	)))

FORM 74.20

Courts of Justice Act

CERTIFICATE OF APPOINTMENT OF ESTATE TRUSTEE WITHOUT A WILL

ONTARIO   *(Court file no.)*

SUPERIOR COURT OF JUSTICE

IN THE ESTATE OF FRANK REID   *(insert name)*, deceased,

late of THE CITY OF TORONTO, ONTARIO

occupation CLERK

who died on JUNE 4, 20--

CERTIFICATE OF APPOINTMENT OF ESTATE TRUSTEE WITHOUT A WILL

Applicant	Address	Occupation
WILLIAM REID	517 BLACK AVENUE CITY OF TORONTO, ONTARIO	TEACHER

This CERTIFICATE OF APPOINTMENT OF ESTATE TRUSTEE WITHOUT A WILL is hereby issued under the seal of the court to the applicant named above.

DATE JUNE 20, 20--

Registrar
Address of court office
330 UNIVERSITY AVENUE, 7TH FLOOR
TORONTO, ONTARIO
M5G 1R7

RCP-E 74.20 (November 1, 2005)
SELF-COUNSEL PRESS-PROBATE-ONT (FORM 74.20) (19-1)07

Court file no.

ONTARIO
SUPERIOR COURT OF JUSTICE
at

IN THE ESTATE OF

FRANK REID , deceased.

**CERTIFICATE OF
APPOINTMENT
OF ESTATE TRUSTEE
WITHOUT A WILL**
(Form 74.20 under the Rules)
JANUARY 1995

*Name, address, telephone number and fax number of
solicitor or applicant:*

WILLIAM REID
517 BLACK AVENUE
TORONTO, ONTARIO

8

Making the Actual Transfers

1. General

You have now reached the stage where you have your Certificate of Appointment of Estate Trustee.

The major task remaining is to transfer the assets to those individuals who are entitled to receive them, whether under the terms of a will or in accordance with the intestacy provisions of the *Succession Law Reform Act*.

Outstanding debts must also be cleared up at this point and outstanding income tax returns must be filed.

As suggested previously, it is probably advisable to advertise for creditors in all situations, although strictly there may not be any obligation to do so. If a personal representative distributes the assets of the estate to the beneficiaries without advertising, he or she will be personally liable if there are any unpaid creditors of the deceased outstanding.

We shall now consider various assets that will be encountered in the administration of an estate and outline the fashion in which they should be dealt with.

2. Real Estate

To properly transfer real estate or any other interest in land such as mortgages and agreements for sale that were registered wholly or partly in the name of the deceased person, certain registrations must be carried out in the appropriate land registry office. This is a more complicated aspect of probate, and you may want to use the services of a lawyer for any real estate transfers.

Each county or district in the province is responsible for its own land registry office and, in most counties, there are at least two offices: one for registration under the *Land Titles Act* and the other for registration under the *Registry Act*. The reasons for the existence of two systems is historical in nature.

These offices are located in the particular county or district in which you are dealing. The office where your property is registered can be ascertained from the legal description found on the deed or mortgage for the property. If you are still uncertain, the staff of the land registry office will generally be pleased to advise you on the proper office for completing these registrations.

Documents that are intended for registration in the land registry office of a particular county or district can be mailed to the land registrar of the county or district; it is not necessary that you personally attend to carry out registrations, but it is a good idea in case the registration clerk requires any corrections to be made to the documents.

The documents you wish to register must be accompanied by a certified cheque payable to the Minister of Finance. The registration fee for a deed (exclusive of land transfer tax) is $60. The cost of registration of the Certificate of Appointment of Estate Trustee is also $60.

2.1 Transferring real estate under the *Registry Act*

To transfer real estate under the *Registry Act* system, you must complete a Transfer/ Deed of Land and attach a schedule that sets out the executor's authority (see Sample 23).

As well as the registration of this deed and schedule, it is also necessary for a notarized copy of the Certificate of Appointment to be registered. A notarized copy consists of two documents:

(a) A photocopy of the original Certificate of Appointment (see Sample 13 in Chapter 6 and the original will)

SAMPLE 23
TRANSFER/DEED OF LAND

<table>
<tr><td colspan="2" rowspan="3">Province of Ontario</td><td colspan="4" align="center">Transfer/Deed of Land
A</td></tr>
<tr><td colspan="4" align="center">Form 1 — Land Registration Reform Act</td></tr>
</table>

FOR OFFICE USE ONLY	**(1) Registry [X] Land Titles [ ]** **(2)** Page 1 of pages
	(3) Property Identifier(s) Block Property Additional: See Schedule [ ]
	(4) Consideration NINETY THOUSAND Dollars $ 90,000.00
	(5) Description This is a: Property Division [ ] Property Consolidation [ ]
New Property Identifiers Additional: See Schedule [ ]	Lot 6, plan 453 City of Toronto (formerly city of North York) The Registry Division of the Toronto Registry Office No. 66
Executions Additional: See Schedule [ ]	

(6) This Document Contains:	(a) Redescription New Easement Plan/Sketch [ ]	(b) Schedule for: Description [ ] Parties [ ] Other [ ] Additional	**(7) Interest/Estate Transferred** Fee Simple

(8) Transferor(s) The transferor hereby transfers the land to the transferee and certifies that the transferor is at least eighteen years old and that I am not a spouse.

Name(s)	Signature(s)	Date of Signature Y M D
SMITH, Mary Matilda Estate Trustee of the Estate of John Adams Smith	*Mary Matilda Smith*	20-- 09 16

(9) Spouse(s) of Transferor(s) I hereby consent to this transaction

Name(s)	Signature(s)	Date of Signature Y M D

(10) Transferor(s) Address for service 230 Frost Avenue, Toronto, Ontario

(11) Transferee(s)	Date of Birth Y M D
PEDIGREE, Gordon	1961 07 16

(12) Transferee(s) Address for Service

(13) Transferor(s) The transferor verifies that to the best of the transferor's knowledge and belief, this transfer does not contravene section 50 of the Planning Act.

Date of Signature Y M D		Date of Signature Y M D
Signature	Signature	

Solicitor for Transferor(s) I have explained the effect of section 50 of the Planning Act to the transferor and I have made inquiries of the transferor to determine that this transfer does not contravene that section and based on the information supplied by the transferor, to the best of my knowledge and belief, this transfer does not contravene that section. I am an Ontario solicitor in good standing.

Name and Address of Solicitor Signature Date of Signature Y M D

(14) Solicitor for Transferee(s) I have investigated the title to this land and to abutting land where relevant and I am satisfied that the title records reveal no contravention as set out in subclause 50(22)(c)(ii) of the Planning Act and that to the best of my knowledge and belief this transfer does not contravene section 50 of the Planning Act. I act independently of the solicitor for the transferor(s) and I am an Ontario solicitor in good standing.

Affix Statement by Solicitor for Transferee(s) here if necessary

Name and Address of Solicitor Signature Date of Signature Y M D

(15) Assessment Roll Number of Property	City. Mun. Map Sub. Par.	**FOR OFFICE USE ONLY**	Fees and Tax
(16) Municipal Address of Property] 10 Green Road North York, Ontario Z1P 0G0	**(17) Document prepared by:** MARY MATILDA SMITH 230 Frost Avenue Toronto, Ontario		Registration Fee Land Transfer Tax **Total**

SAMPLE 23 — CONTINUED

 Province of Ontario

Schedule

Form 5 — Land Registration Reform Act

Page _____

S

Additional Property Identifier(s) and/or Other Information

TRANSFER BY ESTATE TRUSTEE — REGISTRY

This is a schedule to a Transfer/Deed of Land hereby expressed to be dated the ____ day of _____, 20--, affecting

    Lot 6, Plan 453
    City of Toronto (formerly city of North York)
    The Registry Division of the Toronto Registry Office No. 66

John Adams Smith

Died on the 1st day of May, 20—

A certificate of Appointment of Estate Trustee with a will was granted to the Transferror by the Supreme Court of Justice at Toronto on the 26th day of May, 20--.

The Certificate of Appointment of Estate Trustee with a will was registered in the Land Registry Office for the Registry Division of Toronto, on the 15th day of September, 20--.

At the time of his death, John Adams Smith was the owner of the land described herein.

For the purpose of paying the debts of the deceased and distributing the Estate, it is necessary to sell the lands.

FOR OFFICE USE ONLY

SELF-COUNSEL PRESS-PROBATE-ONT (16-1)13

(b) A certificate under seal of a notary public that certifies that the copy is identical to the original (see Sample 24)

Further, in order to register the Certificate of Appointment you must attach another form, the Document General, which is used to register various types of documents (see Sample 25). You must also complete an Affidavit of Residence (see Sample 26) and attach it to the Transfer/ Deed before it is submitted for registration. (If the property is being sold to a third party, it is normally the purchaser who completes and attaches this affidavit.)

2.2 Transferring real estate under the *Land Titles Act*

If the property to be transferred is governed by the *Land Titles Act*, a two-step process is required.

First, a transmission application is used to transfer property from the deceased to the executor or administrator of the estate. The transmission application has three parts:

(a) A Document General (This is the same form as used for the *Registry Act* system, discussed above, but it is filled out differently. Sample 27 shows how to fill it out for the *Land Titles* system.)

(b) A notarial copy of Certificate of Appointment of Estate Trustee (see Sample 24)

(c) An affidavit regarding debts of the deceased (see Sample 28)

The notarial copy of the Certificate of Appointment of Estate Trustee and the affidavit regarding debts should be attached to the Document General as schedules. These three forms make up your transmission application.

When the transmission application is registered, the executor or administrator becomes the legal registered owner of the land. He or she then conveys the property to a purchaser by means of a Transfer/ Deed of Land, which sets out the name of the estate and the personal representative as transferor. This is the same form that is used in the *Registry Act* system, but without any schedule attached to it (see Sample 23).

In this registry you will also be required to complete an Affidavit of Residence (see Sample 26). Estate conveyancing under the *Land Titles* system can be quite complicated. If you are uncertain as to how to proceed, you should seek the help of a real estate lawyer.

SAMPLE 24
NOTARIAL CERTIFICATE TRUE COPY

Notarial Certificate True Copy

CANADA
Province of Ontario
To Wit

To all to whom these Presents may come, be seen or known

I, _Norton Notary_____

A Notary Public, in and for the Province of Ontario, by Royal Authority duly appointed, residing

at the _City_____ of _Toronto_____ in said Province, do Certify that the

paper-writing hereto annexed is a true copy of a document produced and shown to me and

purporting to be the original _Certificate of Appointment of Estate Trustee with a Will_____

of _John Adams Smith_____

late of the _City_____ of _Toronto_____ in the _Province_____

of _Ontario_____ deceased, issued out of the Superior Court of Justice at

_Toronto_____ dated _24th May_____, 20 --_____,

and numbered _____ the said copy having been compared by me with the

said original document, an Act whereof being requested I have granted the same under my

Notarial Form and Seal of Office to serve and avail as occasion shall or may require.

In Testimony Whereof I have hereto subscribed my name _Norton Notary_____

and affixed my Notarial Seal of Office at _City of Toronto_____

this _29th_____ day of _May_____, 20 --_____.

SEAL

_____ _Norton Notary_
Notary Public in and for the Province of Ontario.

SELF-COUNSEL PRESS-PROBATE-ONT (20-1)13

SAMPLE 25
DOCUMENT GENERAL (REGISTRY SYSTEM)

<table>
<tr>
<td rowspan="11" style="writing-mode:vertical">FOR OFFICE USE ONLY</td>
<td colspan="2">🛡️ Province of Ontario</td>
<td colspan="2">Document General
Form 4 — Land Registration Reform Act, 1984</td>
<td>D</td>
</tr>
</table>

		Document General Form 4 — Land Registration Reform Act, 1984	**D**

Province of Ontario 🛡️

Document General

Form 4 — Land Registration Reform Act, 1984 **D**

---

(1) Registry [X]   Land Titles [   ] | **(2)** Page 1 of   pages

(3) Property Identifier(s)   Block   Property | Additional: See Schedule [   ]

(4) Nature of Document

Certificate of Appointment of Estate Trustee

(5) Consideration

Dollars $

(6) Description

New Property Identifiers   Additional: See Schedule [   ]

Executions   Additional: See Schedule [   ]

(7) This Document Contains: (a) Redescription New Easement Plan/Sketch   [   ] | (b) Schedule for: Description [   ]   Additional Parties [   ]   Other [   ]

(8) This Document provides as follows:

Continued on Schedule [   ]

(9) This Document relates to instrument number(s)

(10) Party(ies) (Set out Status or Interest)

Name(s)	Signature(s)	Y	M	D
Smith, Mary Matilda		20--	09	15
Estate Trustee of the Estate of John Adams Smith				

(11) Address for service

(12) Party(ies) (Set out Status or Interest)

Name(s)	Signature(s)	Y	M	D

(13) Address for service

(14) Municipal Address of Property | **(15) Document prepared by:**

2300 Finch Avenue West
Toronto, Ontario
Z1P 0G0

FOR OFFICE USE ONLY

Fees and Tax

Registration Fee

Total

SELF-COUNSEL PRESS-PROBATE-ONT (14-1)13

SAMPLE 26
AFFIDAVIT OF RESIDENCE AND OF VALUE OF THE CONSIDERATION

Property Identifier(s) No.

Land Transfer Tax Affidavit
Land Transfer Tax Act

In the Matter of the Conveyance of *(insert brief description of land)* Part Lot 111, Plan 3233, City of Toronto

BY *(print names of all transferors in full)* Mary Matilda Smith

TO *(print names of all transferees in full)* Gordon P. Pedigree

I Gordon P. Pedigree

have personal knowledge of the facts herein deposed to and Make Oath and Say that:

1. I am *(place a clear mark within the square opposite the following paragraph(s) that describe(s) the capacity of the deponents)*:

[   ] (a) the transferee named in the above-described conveyance;

[   ] (b) the authorized agent or solicitor acting in this transaction for the transferee(s);

[X] (c) the President, Vice-President, Secretary, Treasurer, Director or Manager authorized to act for_____
_____ (the transferee(s));

[   ] (d) a transferee and am making this affidavit on my own behalf and on behalf of *(insert name of spouse)*_____
_____ who is my spouse.

[   ] (e) the transferor or an officer authorized to act on behalf of the transferor company and [   ] I am tendering this document for registration and
[   ] no tax is payable on registration of this document.

2. **THE TOTAL CONSIDERATION FOR THIS TRANSACTION IS ALLOCATED AS FOLLOWS:**

(a)	Monies paid or to be paid in cash	$ 65,000.00
(b)	Mortgages (i) Assumed *(principal and interest)*	$ 25,000.00
	(ii) Given back to vendor	$ Nil
(c)	Property transferred in exchange *(detail below in para. 5)*	$ Nil
(d)	Other consideration subject to tax *(detail below)*	$ Nil
(e)	Fair market value of the lands *(see Instruction 2(c))*	$ Nil
(f)	Value of land, building, fixtures and goodwill subject to Land Transfer Tax *(Total of (a) to (e))*	$ 90,000.00
(g)	Value of all chattels — items of tangible personal property	$ Nil
(h)	Other consideration for transaction not included in (f) or (g) above	$ Nil
(i)	Total Consideration	$ 90,000.00

All blanks
must be filled in.
Insert "Nil"
where applicable.

$ 90,000.00

3. To be completed where the value of the consideration for the conveyance exceeds $400,000.00.

I have read and considered the definition of "single family residence" set out in subsection 1(1) of the Act. The land conveyed in the above-described conveyance:

[   ] does not contain a single family residence or contains more than two single family residences;

[   ] contains at least one and not more than two single family residences; or

[   ] contains at least one and not more than two single family residences and the lands are used for other than just residential purposes. The transferee has accordingly apportioned the value of consideration on the basis that the consideration for the single family residence is $_____
and the remainder of the lands are used for_____purposes.

> **Note:** *Subsection 2(1)(b) imposes an additional tax at the rate of one-half of one per cent upon the value of the consideration in excess of $400,000.00 where the conveyance contains at least one and not more than two single family residences and 2(2) allows an apportionment of the consideration where the lands are used for other than just residential purposes.*

4. If consideration is nominal, is the land subject to any encumbrance?   [   ] Yes   [   ] No

5. Other remarks and explanations, if necessary. N/A

Sworn/affirmed before me in the City of Toronto

in the Province of Ontario

this 5th _____ day of November _____, 20 --

Gordon P. Pedigree
Signature(s)

I.M. Commissioner
A Commissioner for taking Affidavits, etc.

Property Information Record

A. Describe nature of instrument: Deed

B. (i) Address of property being conveyed *(if available)* 42 Rose Avenue, Toronto

(ii) Assessment Roll No. *(if available)* 010-000-111

C. Mailing address(es) for future Notices of Assessment under the *Assessment Act* for property being conveyed
42 Rose Avenue, Toronto, Ontario

D. (i) Registration number for last conveyance of property being conveyed *(if available)* 1984101

(ii) Legal description of property conveyed: Same as in D (i) above. [   ] Yes   [   ] No   [   ] Not Known

E. Name(s) and address(es) of each transferee's solicitor: John B. Law, 151 Legal Avenue, Toronto, Ontario

For Land Registry Office Use Only
Registration No.
Registration Date (Year/Month/Day)
/   /
Land Registry Office No.

School Support (Voluntary Election) *(See reverse for explanation)*

	Yes	No
(a) Are all individual transferees Roman Catholic?	[ ]	[ ]
(b) If Yes, do all individual transferees wish to be Roman Catholic Separate School Supporters?	[ ]	[ ]
(c) Do all individual transferees have French Language Education Rights?	[ ]	[ ]
(d) If Yes, do all individual transferees wish to support the French Language School Board *(where established)*?	[ ]	[ ]

Note: As to (c) and (d) the land being transferred will receive French Public School Board Election unless otherwise directed in (a) and (b).

0449 (2010/05)
SELF-COUNSEL PRESS-PROBATE-ONT (9-1)13

Province of Ontario	**Document General**		**D**
	Form 4 — Land Registration Reform Act, 1984		

FOR OFFICE USE ONLY

(1) Registry [ ] Land Titles [ ]	(2) Page 1 of pages

(3) Property Identifier(s)	Block	Property	Additional: See Schedule [ ]

(4) Nature of Document

Transmission Application

(5) Consideration

Dollars $

(6) Description

Parcel 6-1, Section M-453, being Lot 6
Plan M-453, in the City of Toronto.
The Land Titles Division of the Toronto Registry Office (No. 66).

New Property Identifiers

Additional:
See
Schedule [ ]

Executions

Additional:
See
Schedule [ ]

(7) This Document Contains:	(a) Redescription New Easement Plan/Sketch [ ]	(b) Schedule for: Description [ ] Additional Parties [ ] Other [ ]

(8) This Document provides as follows:

I, Mary Matilda Smith, Estate Trustee of the Estate of John Adams Smith, hereby apply to be registered as owner / ~~estate trustee~~ of the land entered as Parcel 6-1, Section M-453, in the city of Toronto.

The evidence in support of this application consists of:

1. Notarial copy of Certificate of Appointment as Estate Trustee in the Estate of John Adams Smith.

2. The Affidavit of Mary Matilda Smith.

Continued on Schedule [ ]

(9) This Document relates to instrument number(s)

(10) Party(ies) (Set out Status or Interest)

Name(s)	Signature(s)	Y	M	D
Smith, John Adams (estate of)	*Mary Matilda Smith*	20--	09	15

(11) Address for service

(12) Party(ies) (Set out Status or Interest)

Name(s)	Signature(s)	Y	M	D

(13) Address for service

(14) Municipal Address of Property	(15) Document prepared by:	Fees and Tax
20 Green Road Toronto, Ontario Z1P 0G0	2300 Finch Avenue West Toronto, Ontario Z1P 0G0	**FOR OFFICE USE ONLY** Registration Fee / Total

SELF-COUNSEL PRESS-PROBATE-ONT (14-1)13

SCHEDULE 2

IN THE MATTER OF THE ESTATE OF JOHN ADAMS SMITH
LATE OF THE CITY OF TORONTO

A F F I D A V I T

I, MARY MATILDA SMITH, of the City of Toronto, make oath and say:

1. That I am the Estate Trustee of the Estate of John Adams Smith, who died on the 1st day of March, 20--.

2. That the creditors of the deceased, John Adams Smith, have been notified, and all of the debts of the deceased have been paid.

SWORN before me in the City	)
of Toronto, in the Province of	)
Ontario, this 15th day of	) *Mary Matilda Smith*
October 20--.	) MARY MATILDA SMITH
	)
I. M. Commissioner	)
A Commissioner, etc.	)

Several counties in the Province of Ontario no longer use paper documents to transfer ownership of real estate. Transfers of property are done electronically in these counties with the use of a special computer program called Teranet. For security purposes, access to Teranet is limited to registered users who must use special security disks and passwords to access the system. At the date of publication of this book the following jurisdictions required all documents to be registered electronically: Middlesex (London), Halton (Milton), Wentworth (Hamilton), Peel (Brampton), Dufferin (Orangeville), York (Newmarket), Durham (Whitby), Ottawa-Carleton (Ottawa), Simcoe (Barrie), Wellington (Guelph), Brant (Brantford), and Toronto. Expansion of this service will continue across the province so check with your local land registration office to see if your jurisdiction is soon to be or already is included. If the property that you wish to have transferred is located within an electronic registration area, you should seek the assistance of a lawyer or paralegal who is a registered user of the electronic registration system.

3. Mortgages

If one of the assets of the estate of the deceased is a mortgage which he or she held on real property, it will be necessary to transfer this mortgage to the appropriate beneficiary or next-of-kin.

As an alternative, it may be that the personal representative of the estate wishes to sell the mortgage to an outside party.

In any of these events, the transfer of the mortgage is carried out by way of a document known as an Assignment of Mortgage. This document is signed by the personal representative and is registered in the appropriate land registry office for the county or district in which the land mortgaged is located.

If the estate with which you are dealing includes a mortgage, it will probably be necessary for you to obtain the services of a lawyer for the purpose of drawing up the necessary Assignment of Mortgage and having it properly executed and registered.

As we have suggested throughout this book, there is no reason why a lawyer's services cannot be used for various isolated functions throughout the administration of the estate. Although some legal fees will be incurred, this procedure will keep such fees to a minimum, the lawyer performing only those functions that require some special skill, knowledge, or training.

Once again, it will be necessary for you to register in the appropriate land registry office a notarial copy of the Certificate of Appointment of Estate Trustee.

The purpose of registering the Certificate of Appointment of Estate Trustee is, of course, to establish to anyone later searching title to the property that the individual who signed the Assignment of Mortgage had the authority to do so, having been appointed by the appropriate court to act as administrator or executor of the estate.

4. Debts Owing to the Deceased

The collection of any amounts which were owed to the deceased at the time of his or her death is a rather simple procedure for the personal representative of the estate.

It is only necessary for you to establish to the debtor in question that you are entitled to collect the money on behalf of the estate.

To establish this right, it will normally only be necessary for you to produce to the debtor a notarial copy of the Certificate of Appointment of Estate Trustee.

These documents, of course, establish the right and capacity of the personal representative to stand in the shoes of the deceased person.

Needless to say, any contractual arrangements made by the deceased with respect to amounts payable and payment dates will govern the personal representative.

Outstanding indebtedness does not automatically fall due on account of the fact that the creditor dies. Accordingly, if a promissory note does not fall due until a date which happens to be six months after the death of the deceased, you cannot demand payment at once. You are governed by the arrangements that the deceased had made prior to death and will have to await the due date in order to collect the amount in question.

Finally, it should be said that as personal representative you have a right to sue any debtor who does not perform his or her contractual obligations or pay indebtedness which is owing to the deceased.

For these purposes, you step into the shoes of the deceased person and can maintain a legal action for any amounts that he or she is unable to collect.

5. Stocks and Non-Government Bonds

The transfer of stocks and non-government bonds from the name of a deceased to the beneficiary under a will or the next-of-kin (in the case of an intestacy) follows a similar procedure.

First, examine the share certificate or bond in question in order to get the name of the transfer agent for the company whose stocks or bonds are held in the deceased's name.

This information will be readily ascertained from the certificate and will generally be one of the larger trust companies. It is to this transfer agent that the necessary documentation is to be sent. If you have any difficulty finding the name and address of the transfer agent, a stock broker or bond dealer would be able to provide this information. Once you have the name of the transfer agent, you should telephone to determine if there are any special requirements for transferring the stocks or bonds in question.

The following forms or documents are usually required to be sent to the transfer agent to effect the necessary transfer:

(a) Notarial copy of Certificate of Appointment of Estate Trustee (often, too, the transfer agent will ask to examine the original Certificate of Appointment)

   To accomplish this, you need to visit your friendly notary once more and have him or her swear the notarial certified copy form (see Sample 24).

(b) The stock certificate or bond in question

(c) Declaration of Transmission form (see Sample 29)

(d) Power of Attorney form (see Samples 30 and 31)

When preparing the Declaration of Transmission and Power of Attorney, it is not essential that you obtain printed forms and fill in the blanks as has been done in the examples contained in this book. If you so choose, you may simply type the whole of the document, including the printed portions. The form of the document is not vital as long as the wording is essentially the same as that contained in the printed form. Suitable changes in wording should be made depending on whether you are transferring stocks or bonds. It should take only a few days for the necessary transfers to be made. The transfer agent will return to you a new share certificate in the name of the appropriate beneficiary or next-of-kin.

SAMPLE 29
DECLARATION OF TRANSMISSION

Declaration of Transmission

IN THE MATTER OF THE Estate of

__John Adams Smith_____, hereinafter referred to as the "Deceased"
(full name of deceased)

late of__42 Rose Avenue, Toronto, Ontario_____

We/I,__Mary Matilda Smith_____
(full names and addresses of Executors or Administrators)

_42 Rose Avenue, Toronto, Ontario_____

_____

being all of the Executor(s)/Administrator(s) of the said Deceased,
DO SOLEMNLY DECLARE THAT:

(1) The said Deceased died at__Toronto_____

on the__1st_____day of__March_____, 20 --_____ ,

[testate] or ~~[intestate]~~ and at the date of death was domiciled at__42 Rose Avenue,_____

_in the city of Toronto_____

(2) Letters Probate of the Will (~~or Letters of Administration with Will annexed or Letters~~
~~of Administration to the estate~~) of the Deceased were granted to the declarant(s)_____
_Mary Matilda Smith_____

on the__23rd_____day of__July_____, 20 --_____ .

by the__Ontario Court (General Division)_____Court of__the Judicial District of York_____ ,
(full name of Court)

(3) There are registered securities in the name of the Deceased on the register of_____

_Bell Canada_____
(full name of Company)

$_10,000.00_____%_____Bond/Debentures due_____

represented by Bond(s)/Debenture(s) numbered__12821-12830_____

(4) The said__John Adams Smith_____
(full name)

and_____named in the said
(name of Bond(s))

Bond(s)/Debenture(s) was one and the same person.

(5) All of the aforementioned Bond/Debentures were at the date of death physically held

at

_Bigge Bank, Toronto_____

and owned by the said deceased.

(6) By virtue of the foregoing the said Bond(s)/Debenture(s) have devolved upon and
become vested in the Executor(s), Administrator(s) as aforesaid, who desire(s) to have
the same recorded in the names of the Executor(s), Administrator(s) as aforesaid upon
the register of the said Company.
AND THEN

And We/I make this solemn Declaration conscientiously believing it to be true, and
knowing that it is of the same force and effect as if made under oath and by virtue of *The
Canada Evidence Act.*

DECLARED before me at__Toronto_____   _Mary Matilda Smith_____

in the_Province_____of_Ontario_____   Signature of Declarant(s)

this__30th_____day of__July_____

A.D. 20 --_____

_____A. Commissioner_____
A Commissioner for Oaths or Notary Public

Power of Attorney
(To Transfer Stock)

LET IT BE KNOWN THAT

MARY MATILDA SMITH, Executrix of the Estate of JOHN ADAMS SMITH

FOR VALUE RECEIVED has/have bargained, sold, assigned, and transferred; and by these presents, do bargain, sell, assign, and transfer unto_MARY MATILDA SMITH_

Twelve (12) Shares of the_Common_ STOCK of the _RAINBOW GOLD MINES LTD._

standing in_his_ name on the books of the said_RAINBOW GOLD MINES LTD._ represented by Certificate No._S28618_ herewith,_____

AND_I_ do hereby constitute and appoint_the Secretary of the Company_

_my_ true and lawful Attorney, IRREVOCABLY, for_me_ and in_my_ name and stead but to_my_ use, to sell, assign, transfer, and make over all and any part of the said stock, and for that purpose to make and execute all necessary acts of assignment and transfer thereof and to substitute one or more persons with like full power, hereby ratifying and confirming all that said Attorney or_____ substitute or substitutes shall lawfully do by virtue hereof.

IN WITNESS WHEREOF_I_ have hereunto set_my_ hand and seal at_Toronto_ the_23rd_ day of_July_, 20_--_.

Signed, Sealed and Delivered in
the presence of

_____

_____
Signature

POWER OF ATTORNEY (TO TRANSFER BONDS)

Power of Attorney
(To Transfer Bonds)

LET IT BE KNOWN THAT

__MARY MATILDA SMITH, Executrix of the Estate of JOHN ADAMS SMITH_____

FOR VALUE RECEIVED has/have bargained, sold, assigned, and transferred; and by

these presents, do bargain, sell, assign, and transfer unto__MARY MATILDA SMITH___

_____ %_____ Mortgage__10_____

Bonds of__Bell Canada_____ of $__1,000.00_____ each

Nos.__12821-12830_____ amounting to $__10,000.00_____

Registered in__his____ name on the books of the said__Bell Canada_____

AND__I_____ do hereby constitute and appoint__the Secretary of_____

__The Company_____

__my___ true and lawful Attorney, IRREVOCABLY, for__me___ and in__my__ name and stead

but to__my__ use, to sell, assign, transfer, and make over all and any part of the said

bonds, and for that purpose to make and execute all necessary acts of assignment and

transfer thereof and to substitute one or more persons with like full power, hereby

ratifying and confirming all that__my___said Attorney or__his___ substitute or substitutes

shall lawfully do by virtue hereof.

IN WITNESS WHEREOF__I_____ have hereunto set__my_____ hand and seal

at__Toronto_____ the__25ᵗʰ___ day of__July_____, 20__--____

Signed, Sealed, and Delivered in the presence of

_____ _I.M. Witness_____   _____Mary Matilda Smith_____

_____   _____

A small charge for transferring the bonds or stocks into the name of the beneficiary or next-of-kin will often be made.

6. Government Bonds

The procedure for transferring government bonds is somewhat different than for non-government bonds.

It is rare to find provincial or municipal bonds when administering an estate. However, Canada Savings Bonds and other Government of Canada bonds are commonly found as estate assets.

The transfer is carried out by personally visiting the offices of the Bank of Canada or mailing to the Bank of Canada the necessary documentation. If you are dealing only with Canada Savings Bonds, not other government bonds, you can deal directly with the office of Canada Savings Bonds by telephone at 1-800-575-5151 or online at www.csb.gc.ca.

The following forms or documents are required to effect the transfer of Canada Savings Bonds or registered Government of Canada bonds:

(a) Notarial copy of Certificate of Appointment of Estate Trustee (again, you may be asked for the original Certificate of Appointment, so you would be wise to take it along as well)

(b) The bond certificate itself

(c) Estate Transfer Form (2351) (This document serves as the transfer and assignment of the ownership of the bond in question. See Sample 32.)

(d) Affidavit or letter signed by personal representative with respect to name differences (This document is necessary only where the name of the deceased as shown in the Certificate of Appointment of Estate Trustee differs from the name as shown on the bond certificate. The affidavit or letter should simply state that the individual named in the bond certificate and that named in the Certificate of Appointment of Estate Trustee are one and the same person.)

One additional complication exists, however, when dealing with government bonds. It is necessary to have the signature of the es-

SAMPLE 32
ESTATE TRANSFER FORM 2351 — BOND TRANSFERS

Canada Saving Bonds
The way to save guaranteed

Estate Transfer Form (2351)

ETRF-07-10
Protected B (when completed)

SPECIFIC INSTRUCTIONS

This form is used for all provinces except Quebec.
Please print clearly or type the required information into the form fields. Please be sure to complete all required Sections to avoid delays in processing your request. Sign page 3 and mail your request to the destination indicated on page 3.

SECTION A – DETAILS REGARDING THE DECEASED AND THEIR REPRESENTATIVES

JOHN EDWARD JONES

Full name of the deceased (list all variations seen within the legal documents. e.g., Death Certificate, Last Will and Testament, Codicil(s))

### ### ###	20--/01/20	1444 LOGAN STREET			
Social Insurance Number	Date of death (yyyy/mm/dd)	Last address for the deceased			

Civil Status
[ ] Single
[ ] Married
[X] Other, please specify (e.g., divorce, widow) WIDOWER

TORONTO	ON	M5M 5M5	CANADA
City	Prov	Postal code	Country

I / We MARY MATILDA SMITH

Insert full name of all authorized representatives for the deceased
(e.g., spouse, legal estate representative(s), liquidator(s)/executor(s), court appointed administrator(s)/executor(s))

of	42 ROSE AVENUE	TORONTO	ON	M6M 6M6	CANADA
	Care of address (for estate purposes)	City	Prov	Postal code	Country

do solemnly declare as follows,   [X] Administrator / Executor(s)
I am / we are the   [ ] Other, please specify (e.g., spouse) [   ] of the deceased named above.

SECTION B – BOND(S)/PLAN(S) DETAILS

The following is a list of all Government of Canada securities (bonds/plans) which were registered to the deceased at the time of death.

If space is insufficient, please complete and attach a separate sheet that includes the fields seen below. Please initial all attached sheets.

Canada Savings Bonds/ Canada Premium Bonds	Name(s) appearing on the bond(s)		Registration Account # or Certificate Bond Serial #(s)		$ par value
	CANADA SAVINGS BONDS	AND	S293721 - 50	AND	6,000.00
		AND		AND	

-The Registration Account # is 10 digits and can be found on a statement or T5.
- The Bond Serial # is located on the top center of the certificate (e.g., CS101F1234567J).

	Total par value $	6,000.00

[ ] I have attached the physical unsigned certificates to this request.

AND/OR

Payroll Savings Program	Name(s) appearing on the Plan		Plan # (10 digits)
		AND	2

- The 10 digit Plan # can be found on an annual statement or T5.

AND OR

Canada RSP / Canada RIF	Name appearing on the Plan	Plan # (up to 11 digits)

- The Canada RSP plan number is located on the semi-annual statements
- The Canada RIF plan number is located on the quarterly statements

SELF-COUNSEL PRESS-PROBATE-ONT (24-1)13

Canada Saving Bonds
The way to save guaranteed

Estate Transfer Form (2351)

ETRF-07-10
Protected B (when completed)

SECTION C – LETTERS PROBATE OR LETTERS OF ADMINISTRATION

[X]   Select this box only if the following situation applies;

Letters Probate / Letters of Administration were obtained and I am / we are the estate's legal representative(s).
The original or a notarial certified copy of the Letters Probate with a copy of the Will attached or Letters of Administration
(with a copy of the Will attached if applicable) issued by the court has been submitted with this request.

SECTION D – TESTATE (DIED WITH A WILL)

[ ]   Select this box and complete the section below only if the following situation applies;

The deceased left a Last Will dated [   ] which was neither amended nor revoked and no application for
(yyyy/mm/dd)

Letters Probate for the estate has been made or is intended to be made in any jurisdiction.
A notarial certified copy of the deceased Will and Proof of Death that is acceptable to the Bank of Canada is attached.
The following are all the persons, besides myself / ourselves, who are entitled to a share of the securities according to the
Last Will and have consented to the transfer / redemption of the securities by signing below:

Name of the beneficiary		Name of the beneficiary	
Relationship to deceased	Age (if minor)	Relationship to deceased	Age (if minor)
Signature of the beneficiary	WITNESS must sign here	Signature of the beneficiary	WITNESS must sign here

All signatures must be witnessed and the signatories must be of full age of maturity, qualified and duly authorized (submit tutorship or curatorship documents if necessary). If space is insufficient, please complete and attach a separate sheet that includes the fields seen above. Please initial all attached sheets.

SECTION E – INTESTATE (DIED WITHOUT A WILL)

[ ]   Select this box and complete the section below only if the following situation applies;

The deceased dies intestate (without leaving a Last Will and Testament and no application for Letters of Administration for
the estate has been made or is intended to be made in any jurisdiction.
Attached is a Proof of Death that is acceptable to the Bank of Canada.
The following are all the persons, who are entitled to a distributed share of the securities under the laws respecting
intestacy of the Province in which the deceased was domiciled at the time of death and have consented to the transfer /
redemption of the securities by signing below:

Name of the heir		Name of the heir	
Relationship to deceased	Age (if minor)	Relationship to deceased	Age (if minor)
Signature of the heir	WITNESS must sign here	Signature of the heir	WITNESS must sign here

All signatures must be witnessed and the signatories must be of full age of maturity, qualified and duly authorized (submit tutorship or curatorship documents if necessary). If space is insufficient, please complete and attach a separate sheet that includes the fields seen above. Please initial all attached sheets.

SELF-COUNSEL PRESS-PROBATE-ONT (24-2)13

SAMPLE 32 — CONTINUED

Canada Saving Bonds
The way to save guaranteed

Estate Transfer Form (2351)

ETRF-07-10
Protected B (when completed)

SECTION F – FINAL DECLARATION

In consideration of the transfer of redemption of the securities as requested, I / we undertake to indemnify and save harmless the Bank of Canada against any claim that should at any time arise as a result of such transfer or redemption.
I / we further undertake to administer and utilize the share of each beneficiary or heir only in accordance with the law.
By virtue of the foregoing it is requested that the securities be [   ] **Transferred** and/or [X] **Redeemed** in favour of the following:

MARY MATILDA SMITH

Enter the exact names that are to appear on the NEW bonds/plans or cheque payment (continue on next line if required)

[   ] add **"and Survivor"**

Preferred Language of Communication [X] English [ ] French	### ### ### Social Insurance Number (required by income tax legislation)	20--/11/16 Date of birth (yyyy/mm/dd)	S293721 - 50 Series	$6,000.00 $ par value

Care of (if applicable)			Address	
City	Prov	Postal code	Country	Home phone (including area code)	Work phone (including area code)

If more than one beneficiary/heir, please complete and attach a separate sheet that includes the fields seen above. Please initial all attachments.

All debts of the estate have been or will be fully paid; I / we hereby undertake to be responsible for the same to the extent of the amount of the above mentioned securities.
I / we give all right, title, and interest in the securities described above absolutely and the Bank of Canada is hereby authorized to make such entries in the books of registration as are required to give effect to such transfer/redemption.
I / we make this solemn declaration conscientiously believing it to be true and knowing that it is of the same force and effect as if made under oath and by virtue of the Canada Evidence Act.

	TORONTO		20--/02/19
Declared before me at	City	on	Date (yyyy/mm/dd)

FINANCIAL INSTITUTION	Signature of all the authorized representative(s) must be guaranteed by either.	NOTARY PUBLIC
	A Canadian Financial Institution acceptable to the Bank of Canada or by a member of the Medallion guarantee program.	
	OR	
	Witnessed by a Notary Public, properly identified with the Notary Stamp and Signature of the Notary present.	

Note: The "endorsement guaranteed stamp" is NOT acceptable.

Signature of a Notary Public properly identified above

Signature of legal estate representative	Signature of legal estate representative	Signature of legal estate representative

Note: Any alterations should be initialed, by the estate representative(s) before the declaration is signed.

Once fully completed, please mail the form, the legal documents and the unsigned physical certificate bonds (if applicable) to Canada Savings Bonds, Transfer and Exchange, PO BOX 2770, STN D., Ottawa, ON K1P 1J7.

For inquiries, contact us by phone at 1 800 575-5151 or at 1 888 646-2626 for Financial Institution, Monday to Friday from 8 a.m. to 8 p.m. ET. We can also be contacted by TTY (teletypewriter only) at 1 800 354-2222.

Please visit us online at www.cbs.gc.ca.

The personal information provided on this form is protected under the provisions of the PRIVACY ACT and will be used solely for the purpose for which it was collected.

SELF-COUNSEL PRESS-PROBATE-ONT (24-3)13

tate trustee or personal representative on the Estate Transfer Form guaranteed (or witnessed) by a bank or other financial institution.

This, in essence, amounts to having your bank manager sign the document as a witness to your signature confirming that you are, indeed, the person you purport to be. (This shouldn't be a problem.)

One final alternative should be pointed out. Canada Savings Bonds that were owned by the deceased can be surrendered at the Bank of Canada or any chartered bank for their cash value plus accrued interest rather than transferred into the name of the beneficiary or next-of-kin.

This is not possible in the case of registered Government of Canada bonds. It is important to make this distinction. It will be readily ascertainable from the bond certificate itself which type of bond you are dealing with.

The Government of Canada bonds cannot be surrendered for their face value until maturity. If the bonds do not mature for some period of time, it is possible only to transfer them into the name of the beneficiary, or, in the alternative, transfer them into a Government of Canada bearer bond, which can then be sold on the open market.

This latter step may be redundant because, of course, it is possible to sell the Government of Canada bond in its existing form once it has been transferred into the name of the beneficiary or next-of-kin.

If interest rates on this type of bond are lower than current market interest rates, you will face selling the bonds at a discounted price.

7. Bank Accounts

Armed with the original Certificate of Appointment of Estate Trustee and a notarial copy, you should arrange an appointment with the bank manager of the branch where the account is located and present these various documents to him or her.

Any other forms that are required by the particular bank will be provided by the branch manager and it should be a simple matter to attend to the closing of any such account at one meeting.

Dealings with credit unions proceed along similar lines and it is unlikely that you will experience any difficulty in attempting to close out a credit union account. Some credit unions pay out double the amount on deposit because each deposit is life insured automatically.

Certainly, if any additional documentation is required, the credit union or bank in question will provide you with the forms or documents it requires.

8. Automobiles

It is a relatively simple matter to transfer the ownership of an automobile registered in the name of the deceased to a beneficiary or next-of-kin. The ownership card provides a place where details of the transfer of the ownership of the automobile can be completed for the purposes of effecting a change in the motor vehicle records.

Although this portion of the ownership form is usually used for transfers that take place at the time of a sale of the vehicle, it is also used when an owner has died and the automobile is being transferred to a beneficiary or next-of-kin.

Fill in this portion of the ownership form and sign the document indicating your capacity as estate trustee.

It is also necessary for insurance coverage to be arranged prior to effecting the transfer. It will be necessary to establish to the motor vehicle licence bureau at the time of attempting to transfer the ownership that insurance coverage exists.

Accordingly, you should obtain a copy of the usual "pink card" issued by automobile insurers in order to have proof of insurance coverage.

Normally a safety standards certificate is required to transfer the ownership. However, if a transfer is to a spouse, no such certificate is required.

The transfer can be carried out at any of the many motor vehicle licence bureaus spread throughout the province. A nominal fee will be charged for carrying out the transfer of ownership.

9. Life Insurance Policies

If a life insurance policy is payable to the estate it will be necessary to surrender a notarial copy of the Certificate of Appointment of Estate Trustee.

In order to ascertain what other requirements a particular insurance company might have, simply telephone the company or the insurance agent through whom the policy was arranged by the deceased. Generally a Proof of Death form will have to be completed. In addition, the companies generally request the return of the life insurance policy itself.

10. Miscellaneous Items

The transfer of household goods and furniture, jewellery, and other such items is carried out simply by means of a physical delivery of the items to the beneficiary or next-of-kin.

11. Cash on Hand

To handle any cash or cheques that are on hand at the time of death or cheques that may come in following the death, a bank account in the name of the estate should be opened.

This is done simply by going to any local bank or trust company and providing it with a notarial copy of the Certificate of Appointment of Estate Trustee, which will establish your right to deal with the assets of the estate.

Money that comes into your possession can then simply be deposited into this account and drawn out by cheques signed by you in your capacity as the personal representative.

12. Release of Executor or Administrator (Estate Trustee)

When assets of the estate are transferred to beneficiaries, have each beneficiary sign a Release of Executor. By signing this form, the beneficiaries acknowledge receipt of the money or assets transferred to them, release the executor from any further claims, and are prevented from later claiming that they did not receive all of the money or assets to which they were entitled. A similar form, Release of Administrator, is available for estates where the deceased did not leave a will. The release should be signed by each beneficiary in the presence of a witness and an Affidavit of Witness should be completed and sworn by the witness. Examples of these forms are shown in Sample 33 and Sample 34.

Release of Executor

LET IT BE KNOWN THAT

I, _JOHN JONES_

(full legal name)

of _the City of Barrie_ , _in the County of Simcoe, Ontario_

(city/town)   *(province/territory)*

DO HEREBY ACKNOWLEDGE that I have this day had and received of and from

MARY MATILDA SMITH , Executor of the last Will and Testament of

(name of executor)

JOHN ADAMS SMITH , deceased; of _Toronto_ ,

(named of deceased)   *(city/town)*

Ontario , the sum of _One Thousand Dollars (1,000.00)_

(province/territory)

in full satisfaction and payment of such sum or sums of money, legacies, and bequests as are given and bequeathed to me under the last Will and Testament aforesaid and all interest accrued thereon.

AND THEREFORE I, the said _JOHN JONES_

do by these presents, remise, release, quit claim, and forever discharge the said

MARY MATILDA SMITH his/her heirs, executors and administrators of and

(name of executor)

from any and all actions, claims, accounts, and demands whatsoever which I now have or ever had against the aforesaid in respect of or in connection with the Estate of the deceased.

IN WITNESS WHEREOF I have hereunto set my hand and seal
this _25th_ day of _October_ , 20 _--_ .

SIGNED, SEALED, AND DELIVERED
in the presence of

_____

_____
John Jones
signature

SELF-COUNSEL PRESS-PROBATE-ONT (25-1)13

SAMPLE 34
RELEASE OF ADMINISTRATOR

Release of Administrator

LET IT BE KNOWN THAT

I, __JOHN REID_____
                        (full legal name)

of __the City of Toronto_____ , __in the Province of Ontario_____
            (city/town)   *(province/territory)*

DO HEREBY ACKNOWLEDGE that I have this day had and received of and from

__WILLIAM REID_____ , Administrator of the Estate of __FRANK REID_____ ,
   (name of administrator)   *(named of deceased)*

deceased; of __the City of Toronto_____ , __in the Province of Ontario_____ ,
                   (city/town)   *(province/territory)*

the sum of __Fifty-six Thousand, Two Hundred and Twelve Dollars ($56,212.00)_____

in full satisfaction and payment of my distributive share of the said Estate to which I am
entitled under the administration of the said Estate and all interest accrued thereon.

AND THEREFORE I, the said __JEAN REID_____
do by these presents, remise, release, quit claim, and forever discharge the said

__WILLIAM REID_____ his/~~her~~ heirs, executors and administrators of and
        (name of administrator)

from any and all actions, claims, accounts, and demands whatsoever which I now have
or ever had against the aforesaid in respect of or in connection with the Estate.

IN WITNESS WHEREOF I have hereunto set my hand and seal
this __26th_____ day of __October_____, 20 __-- __ .

SIGNED, SEALED, AND DELIVERED
In the presence of

_____   _____
                                        John Reid
                                         signature

SELF-COUNSEL PRESS-PROBATE-ONT (26-1)13

9

Solving Tax Problems

1. Capital Gains Tax

A capital gains tax is a tax based on the amount of profit (or gain) made by a person at the time of his or her disposing of an asset. For example, if you bought ten shares of Bell Canada in July 2000 for $420 (including brokerage charges) and sold those ten shares in March 2002 for $460 (after deducting brokerage charges), you made a capital gain of $40.

You must declare this gain in the tax return filed for the year in which the property was sold. Under the law, one-half of all capital gains are added to any other income of yours and taxed.

If you were an employee making $20,000 salary in 2002, you would commence tax calculations by adding to this employment income $20, this being one-half of the capital gain. From this total of $20,020 you would make deductions and apply the rates to calculate the tax payable.

Though a capital gain is normally experienced (and taxed) only when an asset is sold or given away, the *Income Tax Act* provides for the imposition of tax when the individual dies. This is referred to as a "deemed disposition."

Had you sold the shares of Bell Canada for $400 (after deducting brokerage charges), you would have suffered a "capital loss" of $20. A capital loss is the reverse of a capital gain, being the loss experienced upon the sale of an asset.

In this situation, one-half of the capital loss (or $10) can be deducted from other income when calculating the income tax payable for the year. There are limitations on the amount of capital losses that may be deducted in any one year.

2. When Do You Have to File?

One of your many duties as personal representative is to file the income tax return for the deceased person for the year of his or her death, along with any other returns not yet filed.

For the year of death, the return must be filed either by April 30 of the following year or within six months after the date of death, whichever is later.

Returns not yet filed for the taxation year prior to the year of death must be filed by six months after the date of death.

Say, for example, Thomas Taxed died on March 1, 2005. At that time Mr. Taxed had probably not yet filed his 2004 income tax return which was not due until April 30, 2005. You would have had to file the deceased's tax return for the 2004 taxation year by September 1, 2005, and to file the deceased's 2005 tax return (for the part of the year during which he was alive) by April 30, 2006.

3. The Tax Return for the Year of Death

Under the provisions of the *Income Tax Act*, where a taxpayer has died there are various options open to the personal representative to file more than one return for the year of death. This rather strange concept is permitted only in circumstances of death of a taxpayer.

One example of this situation involves the case where a taxpayer is operating an unincorporated business up to the time of his or her death. It is possible under the provisions of the *Income Tax Act* to file a separate tax return for the income from that business for the period from the close of its fiscal year to the time of the taxpayer's death.

As well, there are other opportunities to file separate returns. The advantage of filing separate returns is, of course, that full personal exemptions and charitable deductions can be claimed on each return. The other obvious advantage is that the lower tax rates can be taken advantage of on more than one occasion.

In the majority of instances, however, you will be in the position of filing a single return for the year of death. This is by far the most frequent situation arising.

In filing the return for the year of death, you should provide, along with the tax return, your full name, address, and official position.

Canada Revenue Agency publishes a supplementary guide to assist in the completion of income tax returns of deceased persons. A copy of this publication can be obtained from your local district taxation office. Obviously, you should read this booklet thoroughly before attempting to complete the income tax return for the year of death. It adequately sets forth the necessary changes that have to be made because the return is for a deceased taxpayer.

You would probably be negligent in attempting to complete the return without obtaining this supplementary guide.

4. How to File the Deceased's Income Tax Return

In preparing and filing the deceased's income tax return, you must declare, and pay tax on, gains on all the assets owned by the deceased on the day of death as though the deceased had sold all of his or her assets on that date. Any increase in value over the cost of any of the assets in the estate will result in a capital gain, three-quarters of which is taxable. (See information on capital gains in section 1. of this chapter.)

The *Income Tax Act* provides specifically for an exemption from the imposition of a capital gains tax on death in the case where the property upon which a capital gain has been realized passes to the spouse of the deceased person either under the provisions of a will or on account of the intestacy provisions of the *Succession Law Reform Act*.

Thus, where the whole of the estate passes to the spouse of the deceased, there will be no capital gains tax payable upon the death.

Had the estate been left instead to, say, a brother or anyone other than a spouse, it would be necessary to obtain values for all the assets of the estate and calculate what capital gains and capital losses are involved. Most of the assets of a typical estate are not the type of asset that increases in value. Life insurance policies, bank accounts, Canada Savings Bonds, household furniture, automobiles, mortgages, cash and cheques on hand, amounts owing to the deceased, and the like do not involve any capital gains consequences. Stocks and real estate are likely the only areas where a potential capital gain exists. However, the principal residence of the deceased is exempt from capital gains tax.

5. Valuation Days

When the original provisions concerning capital gains in the *Income Tax Act* were drafted, it was decided that it would be unfair to tax any capital gains made before the law came into effect. Hence, only increases in value which have accrued since that time are subject to a capital gains tax.

For example, if a man acquired 100 acres of vacant land in Muskoka for $1,000 in 1960 and it was appraised at $95,000 on his death in 2000, the capital gain is not measured as $94,000. Rather, it is necessary for you to ascertain the value of the acreage as of December 31, 1971 (the day before the capital gains tax became law). Assume that this value amounted to $80,000. The capital gain for tax purposes is then only $15,000, one-half of which is subject to tax.

For any property acquired after December 31, 1971, the capital gain is measured simply by deducting the actual cost from the value of the property on the date of death. To determine the gain for any property acquired before January 1, 1972, it will be necessary to ascertain the value of that property at the time the capital gains tax came into force. The result is that no capital gains or capital losses resulting prior to January 1, 1972, will be taken into account.

The concept of "valuation day" was devised by the federal government to ensure that this was so. In fact, two valuation days were proclaimed. December 22, 1971, is valuation day for publicly traded stocks and shares, while December 31, 1971, is valuation day for all other property.

In order to measure any capital gain on property acquired before this system began, but sold after, the value of the property as of valuation day must be determined, and this value will generally be deducted from the value at the date of death to determine the capital gains.

Needless to say, the above examples oversimplify the procedure and calculations. There are special rules which apply in situations where property has fluctuated in value over the years rather than simply increasing or decreasing in value in a straight line. The rules are complex. Only in rare circumstances should you attempt to carry through such calculations without legal assistance.

6. The Estate Income Tax Return (T-3)

For the purposes of the *Income Tax Act*, an estate is treated as a person and can, thus, earn income. If the estate has realized income or capital gains from the time of death until the time of disposal of the assets, an income tax return for the estate must be filed. The estate income tax return is really a calculation of tax on income and not on the value of the estate itself.

The form to fill out is called a T-3 and must be completed for any estate that generates income over $500. If all the income is paid out to the beneficiaries in the taxation year (the first fiscal year starts at date of death and ends 12 months later), there will be no tax to pay on the T-3. However, you will have to issue T-3 remittance slips to the various beneficiaries and they would be liable for the tax on the income (not the "corpus" part) received from the estate.

For most do-it-yourselfers, the entire proceeds of the estate would likely be distributed within, say, a year of death. If the estate earned no income during this period, no forms need be filed. If the estate earned more than $500 or paid over $100 of income to any single beneficiary, then the T-3 form must be filled out.

The tax department publishes a useful guide called the T-3 Trust Guide that you should pick up if possible.

10

The Canada Pension Plan

1. Benefits under the Plan

Too often people forget the benefits payable under the Canada Pension Plan arising from the death of a deceased contributor.

Practically all individuals earning income from employment, as well as all self-employed individuals, must contribute to the plan.

Upon the death of any individual who has contributed to the plan for the minimum contributory period, three possible types of benefits are available to those surviving the deceased contributor:

(a) A lump-sum death benefit payable to the estate or the surviving spouse to help offset funeral expenses

(b) A monthly pension payable to a surviving spouse, whether husband or wife, if any

(c) A monthly pension for dependent children, if any

The personal representative of the estate and the surviving spouse and children should carefully consider the potential benefits to see which, if any, are payable in the particular circumstances of the estate with which they are dealing.

The minimum contributory period provided for in the Canada Pension Plan requires contributions to the plan for at least three years and for one-third of the total number of calendar years from January 1, 1966 (or such later date that the deceased became liable to contribute to the plan), to the date of death. Once the deceased has contributed for ten calendar years, he or she will thereafter be deemed to have satisfied the minimum contributory requirements.

2. Lump-Sum Death Benefit

Provided that the deceased individual has contributed to the plan for the minimum contributory period, a lump-sum death benefit will be payable to the estate.

The size of the lump-sum payment will depend on the amount actually contributed to the plan by the deceased. The amount is calculated on the basis of six times the monthly retirement pension that he or she was collecting at the time of death or, in the event that no retirement pension was being collected at that time, on the basis of six times the amount that the monthly retirement pension would have been had the deceased person been eligible for a pension on that date. The lump-sum amount will then be six times this hypothetical retirement pension.

The maximum lump-sum payment by way of death benefit for a death occurring in 2004 was $4,050. This maximum amount is calculated by taking one-tenth of the year's maximum pensionable earnings (i.e., the amount used to calculate contributions to the plan as shown on the annual income tax return) and will increase in subsequent years in accordance with this formula.

Application forms for the lump-sum death benefit and instruction booklets on how to complete the form can be obtained free of charge upon request at the local office of the Canada Pension Plan. These are spread throughout the province.

Various documents must accompany the application. These include:

(a) Death certificate

(b) Deceased's birth certificate

(c) Deceased's social insurance card

If the deceased was receiving Canada Pension Plan payments at the time of his or her death, only the death certificate is required with the application. An Application for Death Benefit is shown in Sample 35.

SAMPLE 35
APPLICATION FOR DEATH BENEFIT

 Service Canada

PROTECTED B (when completed)
Personal Information Bank HRSDC PPU 146

Application for a Canada Pension Plan Death Benefit

It is very important that you:
- send in this form with supporting documents
  (see the information sheet for the documents we need); and
- use a pen and print as clearly as possible.

SECTION A - INFORMATION ABOUT THE DECEASED

1A. Social Insurance Number	1B. Date of Birth YYYY MM DD	1C. Country of Birth (If born in Canada, indicate province or territory)	FOR OFFICE USE ONLY AGE ESTABLISHED
978 654 321	1961 11 21	ONTARIO, CANADA	

2A. Sex	2B. Date of Death *(See the information sheet for a list of acceptable proof of date of death documents)* YYYY MM DD	DATE OF DEATH ESTABLISHED
⊙ Male ◯ Female	20-- 03 01	

3. Marital status at the time of death

(See the information sheet for important information about marital status)

◯ Single   ⊙ Married   ◯ Separated
◯ Common-law   ◯ Divorced   ◯ Surviving spouse or common-law partner

4A.

⊙ Mr.   ◯ Mrs.
◯ Ms.   ◯ Miss

Usual First Name and Initial	Last Name
JOHN A.	SMITH

4B. Full name at birth, if different from 4A.

First Name and Initial	Last Name

4C. Name on social insurance card, if different from 4A.

First Name and Initial	Last Name

5. Home Address at the time of death (No., Street, Apt., R.R.)

	City
42 ROSE AVENUE	TORONTO

Province or Territory	Country other than Canada	Postal Code
ONTARIO	CANADA	M7Y 2B2

6A. If the address shown in number 5 is outside of Canada, indicate the province or territory in which the deceased last resided.

6B. In which year did the deceased leave Canada?

7. Did the deceased ever live or work in another country?

◯ Yes   ⊙ No

If yes, indicate the names of the countries and insurance numbers. (If you need more space, use the space provided on page 4 of this application). Also, indicate whether a benefit has been requested.

	Country	Insurance Number	Has a benefit been requested?
a)			◯ Yes ◯ No
b)			◯ Yes ◯ No
c)			◯ Yes ◯ No

Service Canada delivers Human Resources and Skills Development Canada programs and services for the Government of Canada.

SC ISP-1200 (2012-10-02) E   1 of 5   Disponible en français   Canada

SIN 978 654 321

8A. Did the deceased ever receive or apply for a benefit under the:

Canada Pension Plan? ○ Yes ◉ No

Old Age Security? ○ Yes ◉ No

Régime de rentes du Québec? (Quebec Pension Plan) ○ Yes ◉ No

8B. If yes to any of the above, provide the Social Insurance Number or account number.

9. Was the deceased or the deceased's spouse eligible to receive Family Allowances or was the deceased, the deceased's spouse or the common-law partner eligible to receive the Child Tax Benefit for any children born **after December 31, 1958**?

Deceased contributor ○ Yes ○ No

Deceased's spouse or common-law partner ◉ Yes ○ No

SECTION B - INFORMATION ABOUT THE SETTLEMENT OF THE ESTATE
(See "Who should apply for the Death benefit" on the information sheet)

10. Is there a will?

◉ Yes Please provide the name and address of the executor in number 11 and go to section C.

○ No Go to number 12.

FOR OFFICE USE ONLY	The Estate of

11. ○ Mr. ◉ Mrs. ○ Ms. ○ Miss

First Name and Initial: MARY M.

Last Name: SMITH

Mailing Address (No., Street, Apt., P.O. Box, R.R.): 42 ROSE AVENUE

City: TORONTO

Province or Territory	Country other than Canada	Postal Code
ONTARIO	CANADA	M7Y 2B2

12. There is no will and I am applying for the Death benefit as:

○ an administrator appointed by the court (**Please give your name and address in number 11**)

○ the person responsible for the funeral expenses (**You must submit the funeral contract or funeral receipts with your application.**)

○ the spouse or common-law partner of the deceased

○ the next-of-kin (Please specify your relationship) _____

○ other (Please specify) _____

SECTION C - INFORMATION ABOUT THE APPLICANT

13. ○ Mr. ◉ Mrs. ○ Ms. ○ Miss

First Name and Initial: MARY M.

Last Name: SMITH

14. Relationship of applicant to the deceased: WIFE

Your Language Preference

Written Communications (Check one): ◉ English ○ French

Verbal Communications (Check one): ◉ English ○ French

FOR OFFICE USE ONLY	For the Estate of

Mailing Address (No., Street, Apt., P.O. Box, R.R.): 42 ROSE AVENUE

City: TORONTO

Province or Territory	Country other than Canada	Postal Code
ONTARIO	CANADA	M7Y 2B2

SC ISP-1200 (2012-10-02) E   2 of 5

SIN 978 654 321

SECTION D - APPLICANT'S DECLARATION

I hereby apply on behalf of the estate of the deceased contributor for a Death benefit. I declare that, to the best of my knowledge, the information given in this application is true and complete.

NOTE: If you make a false or misleading statement, you may be subject to an administrative monetary penalty and interest, if any, under the *Canada Pension Plan*, or may be charged with an offence. Any benefits you received or obtained to which there was no entitlement would have to be repaid.

		YYYY MM DD
APPLICANT'S SIGNATURE	*Mary M. Smith*	DATE	20-- 03 15

TELEPHONE NUMBER   416-222-3333

NOTE: We can only accept a signature with a mark (e.g. X) if a **responsible person witnesses it. That person must also complete the declaration below.**

SECTION E - WITNESS'S DECLARATION

If the applicant signs with a mark, a witness (friend, member of the family, etc.) must complete this section. I have read the contents of this application to the applicant, who appeared to fully understand and who made his or her mark in my presence.

Name	Relationship to applicant	Telephone number
Address	Signature	Date YYYY MM DD

FOR OFFICE USE ONLY	
Application taken by: (Please print name and phone number)	Telephone Number
Application approved pursuant to the Canada Pension Plan.	Authorized Signature
	Date

SC ISP-1200 (2012-10-02) E   3 of 5

SIN 978 654 321

Use this space, if needed, to provide us with more information. Please indicate the question number concerned for each answer given. If you need more space, use a separate sheet of paper and attach it to this application.

SC ISP-1200 (2012-10-02) E   4 of 5

3. Survivor's Pension

If the deceased contributor is survived by a spouse, whether male or female, he or she may be eligible for a survivor's pension (see Sample 36).

It is, once again, necessary for the deceased person to have contributed to the plan for the minimum contributory period. The precise amount of the pension depends on a number of factors, including the amount of actual contributions to the plan, the age of the applicant, and the number of dependent children who survive the deceased.

Upon assessing these various factors, a monthly pension amount is arrived at.

Under the Canada Pension Plan, no survivor's pension is payable to a person who was, at the time of the death of the contributor, younger than the age of 35, unless he or she has dependent children or unless he or she is disabled.

Application forms for the survivor's pension and instruction booklets on how to complete the form can be obtained free of charge from the local office of the Canada Pension Plan.

Various documents must accompany the application. These include:

(a) A death certificate

(b) Deceased's birth certificate

(c) Deceased's social insurance card

(d) Marriage certificate

(e) Survivor's birth certificate

(f) Survivor's social insurance card

Three of the required documents duplicate the requirements for the application for a lump-sum death benefit. If both types of benefits are being applied for, it is usual to send in both applications at the same time.

If the deceased and the surviving spouse were both receiving Canada Pension Plan Benefits at the time of death, only the death certificate and the marriage certificate are required with the application.

SAMPLE 36
APPLICATION FOR SURVIVOR'S PENSION

 Service
Canada

Application for a Canada Pension Plan
Survivor's Pension and Child(ren)'s Benefits

It is very important that you:

- send in this form with supporting documents
  (see the information sheet for the documents we need); **and**

- use a **pen** and **print** as clearly as possible.

SECTION A - INFORMATION ABOUT YOUR DECEASED SPOUSE OR COMMON-LAW PARTNER (The deceased contributor)

1A. Social Insurance Number	1B. Date of Birth YYYY MM DD	1C. Country of Birth (If born in Canada, indicate province or territory)	FOR OFFICE USE ONLY
987 654 321	1961 11 21	ONTARIO, CANADA	AGE ESTABLISHED

2A. Sex	2B. Date of Death (See the information sheet for a list of acceptable proof of date of death documents)		DATE OF DEATH ESTABLISHED
◉ Male ◯ Female		YYYY MM DD 20--03 01	

3. Marital status at the time of death
(See the information sheet for important information about marital status)

◯ Single   ◉ Married   ◯ Separated
◯ Common-Law   ◯ Surviving spouse or common-law partner   ◯ Divorced

4A.	Usual First Name and Initial	Last Name
◉ Mr. ◯ Mrs. ◯ Ms. ◯ Miss	JOHN A.	SMITH

4B. Full name at birth, if different from 4A.	First Name and Initial	Last Name

4C. Name on social insurance card, if different from 4A.	First Name and Initial	Last Name

5. Home Address at the time of death (No., Street, Apt., R.R.)

Home Address	City
42 ROSE AVENUE	TORONTO

Province or Territory	Country other than Canada	Postal Code
ONTARIO	CANADA	M7Y 2B2

If the address shown above is outside of Canada, indicate the province or territory in which the deceased last resided.

6. Did your deceased spouse or common-law partner ever live or work in another country?

◉ Yes   ◯ No

If **yes**, indicate the names of the countries and the insurance numbers. (If you need more space, use the space provided on page 6 of this application) Also, indicate whether a benefit has been requested.

	Country	Insurance Number	Has a benefit been requested?
a)			◯ Yes ◯ No
b)			◯ Yes ◯ No
c)			◯ Yes ◯ No

Service Canada delivers Human Resources and Skills Development Canada programs and services for the Government of Canada.

SC ISP-1300 (2013-03-06) E   1 of 7   Disponible en français   Canada

SIN   987 654 321

SECTION B - INFORMATION ABOUT YOU (The surviving spouse or common-law partner)

7A. Social Insurance Number	7B. Date of Birth YYYY MM DD	7C. Country of Birth (If born in Canada, indicate province or territory)	FOR OFFICE USE ONLY AGE ESTABLISHED
978 654 555	1963 02 01	ONTARIO, CANADA	

Your Language Preference	8A. Written Communications (Check one)	8B. Verbal Communications (Check one)
	(●) English ( ) French	(●) English ( ) French

9A. ( ) Mr. (●) Mrs ( ) Ms. ( ) Miss

Usual First Name and Initial MARY M.

Last Name SMITH

9B. Full name at birth, if different from 9A.

First Name and Initial

Last Name

9C. Name on social insurance card, If different from 9A.

First Name and Initial

Last Name

10. Mailing Address (No., Street, Apt., P.O. Box, R.R.) 42 ROSE AVENUE

City TORONTO

Province or Territory	Country other than Canada	Postal Code
ONTARIO	CANADA	M7Y 2B2

Telephone Number(s)	11A. Area code and telephone number at home	11B. Area code and telephone number at work (if applicable)
	416-222-3333	

12. Home Address, if different from mailing address (No., Street, Apt., R.R.)

City

Province or Territory	Country other than Canada	Postal Code

13A. Are you receiving or have you ever applied for a benefit under the:

Canada Pension Plan?	Old Age Security?	Régime de rentes du Québec? (Quebec Pension Plan)
( ) Yes (●) No	( ) Yes (●) No	( ) Yes (●) No

13B. If you answered yes to any of the above, provide the Social Insurance Number or account number under which you applied.

14. Are you disabled? ( ) Yes (●) No

15A. Were you married to the deceased?

(●) Yes   ( ) No

If yes, date of marriage (Please submit your marriage certificate)

YYYY MM DD 1983 06 14

15B. Were you still married at the time of your spouse's death?

(●) Yes   ( ) No

15C. Were you still living together at the time of your spouse's death?

(●) Yes   ( ) No

FOR OFFICE USE ONLY	MARRIAGE ESTABLISHED

16A. If you were the common-law partner of the deceased, when did you start living together?

YYYY MM DD

16B. Were you still living together at the time of your common-law partner's death?

( ) Yes   ( ) No

If yes and you were the common-law partner of the deceased, please obtain and complete the form titled "Statutory Declaration of Common-law Union" and return it with this application.

FOR OFFICE USE ONLY	COMMON-LAW ESTABLISHED

SC ISP-1300 (2013-03-06) E   2 of 7

SIN 987 654 321   PROTECTED B (when completed)

17. If you were under 45 years of age at the time of your spouse's or common-law partner's death, were you responsible for the care of:

a) a child of your deceased spouse or common law partner **under 18 years of age** who was not in your care and custody?   ○ Yes   ◉ No

b) a disabled child of your deceased spouse or common-law partner **over 18 years of age**?   ○ Yes   ◉ No

c) a child of your deceased spouse or common-law partner **between the ages of 18 to 25** in full-time attendance at school or university?   ○ Yes   ◉ No

IF YOU ANSWERED "YES" TO ANY OF THE ABOVE, PLEASE EXPLAIN THE CIRCUMSTANCES IN THE SPACE PROVIDED ON PAGE 6 OF THIS APPLICATION AND INDICATE WHETHER OR NOT YOU ARE STILL CARING FOR THE CHILD.

18. Direct deposit (For Canada only)

For direct deposit outside Canada, please contact us at 1-800-277-9914 (from the United States) and at 613-990-2244 from all other countries (we accept collect calls).

If your application is approved, do you want your monthly payments deposited into your account at your financial institution?

◉ Yes   ○ No (Go to question 19)

If yes, complete the boxes below (you may want to contact your financial institution to get this information).

Branch Number (5 digits)	Institution Number (3 digits)	Account Number (maximum of 12 digits)
_____	_____	_____

Name(s) on the account   Telephone number of your financial institution

You can attach an unsigned personalized cheque with the word "VOID" on the front of the cheque and your social insurance number on the back.

19. Voluntary Income Tax Deduction   **This service is available to Canadian residents only.**

Your Canada Pension Plan benefit is taxable income. If we approve your application, would you like us to deduct **federal income tax** from your monthly payment? *(See the information sheet for more information)*

◉ Yes   ○ No

	Federal Income Tax	Federal Income Tax
If yes, indicate the dollar amount or percentage you want us to deduct each month.	$ _____	_____ %

SECTION C - INFORMATION ABOUT THE CHILD(REN) OF THE DECEASED

20. Do you have any children **under the age of 18**?

◉ Yes   ○ No

If yes, please provide the following information.

a) Child's Usual First Name and Initial   Last Name

JOANNA M.   SMITH

Sex	Date of Birth	YYYY MM DD	Social Insurance Number
○ Male ◉ Female		1997 01 13	123 345 789

Is the child in your care and custody since birth?	Is the child **still** in your care and custody?
◉ Yes ○ No **If no**, please indicate since when: YYYY MM DD	◉ Yes ○ No **If no**, please provide a letter of explanation.

Is the child a:
◉ child of your deceased spouse or common-law partner   ○ legally adopted child of your deceased spouse or common-law partner   ○ other (Explain circumstances in the space provided on page 6 of this application)

FOR OFFICE USE ONLY   AGE ESTABLISHED

SC ISP-1300 (2013-03-06) E   3 of 7

SIN 987 654 321

b) Child's Usual First Name and Initial

PETER T.

Last Name

SMITH

Sex	Date of Birth	YYYY MM DD	Social Insurance Number
◉ Male ◯ Female		1999 04 17	987 789 987

Is the child in your care and custody since birth?

◉ Yes   ◯ No   **If no**, please indicate since when: YYYY MM DD

Is the child **still** in your care and custody?

◉ Yes   ◯ No   **If no**, please provide a letter of explanation.

Is the child a:

◉ child of your deceased spouse or common-law partner

◯ legally adopted child of your deceased spouse or common-law partner

◯ other (Explain circumstances in the space provided on page 6 of this application)

FOR OFFICE USE ONLY	AGE ESTABLISHED

21. Do you have any children **between the ages of 18 and 25** attending school, college or university full-time?

◯ Yes   ◉ No

If yes, please provide the following information.

a) Child's Usual First Name and Initial   Last Name   Date of Birth   YYYY MM DD

Mailing Address (No., Street, Apt., P.O. Box, R.R.)   City

Province or Territory   Country other than Canada   Postal Code

b) Child's Usual First Name and Initial   Last Name   Date of Birth   YYYY MM DD

Mailing Address (No., Street, Apt., P.O. Box, R.R.)   City

Province or Territory   Country other than Canada   Postal Code

22. Are any of the children named in questions 20 and 21 receiving or have they applied for a benefit under:

a) the Canada Pension Plan?   ◯ Yes ◉ No   **b)** Régime de rentes du Québec? (Quebec Pension Plan)   ◯ Yes ◉ No

If **yes**, to either or both, indicate the name of the child(ren) and the Social Insurance Number under which benefits are being received or have been applied for.

Child's Usual First Name and Initial   Social Insurance Number

_____   _____

_____   _____

_____   _____

_____   _____

23. Have you been wholly or substantially maintaining all of the children listed in question 20 and 21, since the death of your spouse or common-law partner?   ◉ Yes   ◯ No   **If no**, please explain on page 6 of this application.

SC ISP-1300 (2013-03-06) E   4 of 7

SAMPLE 36 — CONTINUED

PROTECTED B (when completed)

SECTION D - INFORMATION ABOUT THE APPLICANT
(If not the surviving spouse or common-law partner named in Section B)

24. Social Insurance Number	Your Language Preference	25A. Written Communications (Check one)		25B. Verbal Communications (Check one)	
		○ English	○ French	○ English	○ French

26. ○ Mr. ○ Mrs. ○ Ms. ○ Miss   Usual First Name and Initial   Last Name

27. Mailing Address (No., Street, Apt., P.O. Box, R.R.)   City

Province or Territory   Country other than Canada   Postal Code

Telephone Number(s) | 28A. Area code and telephone number at home | 28B. Area code and telephone number at work (if applicable)

Please explain on a separate sheet of paper why you are making this application

APPLICANT'S DECLARATION

I hereby apply for a Survivor's Pension and/or child(ren)'s benefits under the provisions of the Canada Pension Plan. I declare that, to the best of my knowledge, the information on this application is true and complete. I realize that my personal information is governed by the *Privacy Act* and it can be disclosed where authorized under the Canada Pension Plan.

NOTE: If you make a false or misleading statement, you may be subject to an administrative monetary penalty and interest, if any, under the *Canada Pension Plan*, or may be charged with an offence. Any benefits you received or obtained to which there was no entitlement would have to be repaid.

YYYY MM DD

APPLICANT'S SIGNATURE X   *Mary M. Smith*   DATE   20-- 03 15

NOTE: We can only accept a signature with a mark (e.g. X) if a responsible person witnesses it. That person must also complete the declaration below.

WITNESS'S DECLARATION

If the applicant signs with a mark, a witness (friend, member of the family, etc.) must complete this section.

I have read the contents of this application to the applicant, who appeared to fully understand and who made his or her mark in my presence.

Name   Relationship to applicant   Telephone number

Address   Signature   Date YYYY MM DD

FOR OFFICE USE ONLY

Application taken by: (Please print name and phone number)   Telephone Number

Application approved pursuant to the Canada Pension Plan.   Authorized Signature

Effective Date _____ (month) _____ (year)   Date

SC ISP-1300 (2013-03-06) E   5 of 7

SIN 987 654 321

Use this space, if needed, to provide us with more information. Please indicate the question number concerned for each answer given. If you need more space, use a separate sheet of paper and attach it to this application.

SC ISP-1300 (2013-03-06) E

6 of 7

If husband and wife were divorced prior to the death of the deceased contributor, the former spouse is not eligible for a survivor's pension at all.

If husband and wife were separated prior to the death of the deceased contributor, the surviving spouse is entitled to a survivor's pension as long as he or she was legally married to the deceased and did not release his or her rights in a separation agreement.

Where the deceased was living in a common-law relationship for a period of at least one year prior to his or her death, and the person with whom the deceased was residing was publicly represented as the spouse of the deceased, the administrator of the Canada Pension Plan has the discretion to pay the survivor's pension to the common-law spouse rather than to a legal surviving spouse.

4. Benefits for Dependent Children

Benefits for children are also payable on the death of a contributor.

A child, if he or she qualifies in all other respects, is eligible for a monthly pension even though his or her other parent may still be living.

To be eligible for the benefits payable, the child must be the natural or adopted child of the deceased contributor, younger than the age of 18, or between 18 and 25 if attending school or university full time.

The result of a successful application will be a monthly pension payable to the parent or guardian of the child until he or she attains the age of 18.

If the pension continues after the age of 18 because the child is in full-time attendance at school or university, it is payable directly to the child.

The application form for a survivor's pension (Sample 36) doubles as an application for benefits for children younger than the age of 18.

By filling in additional parts of the form, the two applications are made simultaneously. If application is being made by a child older than the age of 18 years, a separate form is available from the local office of the Canada Pension Plan upon request (see Sample 37).

Additional documents that will be required include:

(a) Birth certificate of each child

(b) Social insurance card for each child (if any)

(c) Declaration of attendance at school (for children older than 18). This form is available from Service Canada at www.servicecanada.gc.ca or 1-800-622-6232.

SAMPLE 37
APPLICATION FOR CHILD'S BENEFIT

 Service Canada

PROTECTED B (when completed)
Personal Information Bank HRSDC PPU 146

Application for a Canada Pension Plan Child's Benefit
(BENEFIT FOR CHILD AGE 18 TO 25 AND IN FULL TIME ATTENDANCE AT SCHOOL OR UNIVERSITY)
THIS APPLICATION MUST BE SUPPORTED BY A DECLARATION OF ATTENDANCE AT SCHOOL OR UNIVERSITY FORM

It is very important that you:
- send in this form with supporting documents (see the information sheet for the documents we need); **and**
- use a **pen** and **print** as clearly as possible.

SECTION A - INFORMATION ABOUT THE CONTRIBUTOR

1A. Contributor's Social Insurance Number	1B. Sex	1C. Preferred language for correspondence
978 654 321	(●) Male ( ) Female	(●) English ( ) French

2. (●) Mr. ( ) Mrs. ( ) Ms. ( ) Miss   Usual First Name and Initial   JOHN A.   Last Name   SMITH

3. Contributor's Address (No., Street, Apt., R.R.)   42 ROSE AVENUE   City   TORONTO

4. Province or Territory	Country other than Canada	Postal Code
ONTARIO	CANADA	M7Y 2B2

SECTION B - INFORMATION ABOUT THE CHILD OF THE CONTRIBUTOR

5A. Child's Social Insurance Number	5B. Sex
234 789 567	(●) Male ( ) Female

6. (●) Mr. ( ) Mrs. ( ) Ms. ( ) Miss   Usual First Name and Initial   STEPHEN A.   Last Name   SMITH

7. Home Address if different from 3 above (No., Street, Apt., R.R.)   308 BERKELEY STREET   City   TORONTO

Province or Territory	Country other than Canada	Postal Code
ONTARIO	CANADA	M2Y 6H4

8. Mailing Address for cheque if different from 7 above (No., Street, Apt., R.R.)   City

Province or Territory	Country other than Canada	Postal Code

9A. Are you disabled?	9B. Date of Birth YYYY MM DD	AGE ESTABLISHED (FOR OFFICE USE ONLY)
( ) Yes (●) No	1995 04 02	

10A. Are or were you ever a beneficiary or an applicant for a benefit under: Canada Pension Plan? ( ) Yes (●) No   Quebec Pension Plan? ( ) Yes (●) No   **10B.** If yes, under what Social Insurance Number

11. Are you a natural or legally adopted child of the contributor?   (●) Yes ( ) No   If legally adopted, indicate date of adoption.   YYYY MM DD

SECTION C - DECLARATION OF APPLICANT

12. I hereby apply for a Disabled Contributor's Child's Benefit. [ ]   I hereby apply for a Surviving Child's Benefit. [✔]

I declare that, to the best of my knowledge and belief, the information given in this application is true and completed and I undertake to notify Service Canada of any changes in the circumstances which may affect eligibility.

NOTE: If you make a false or misleading statement, you may be subject to an administrative monetary penalty and interest, if any, under the *Canada Pension Plan*, or may be charged with an offence. Any benefits you received or obtained to which there was no entitlement would have to be repaid.

Student's Signature	Date of Application YYYY MM DD 20-- 03 16	Telephone Number 416 555 5555

FOR OFFICE USE ONLY - DO NOT WRITE BELOW THIS LINE

Application taken by:		Date Application Received
Application approved pursuant to Subsection 59(3) of the Canada Pension Plan.	Date	
	Authorized Signature	
Effective Date (year) (month)		

Service Canada delivers Human Resources and Skills Development Canada programs and services for the Government of Canada.

SC ISP-1400 (2012-08-30) E   Disponible en français   Canada

Appendix:
Estate Trustee's/
Personal
Representative's
Checklist

1. Take all steps necessary to protect and preserve the deceased's assets.

2. Locate the will.

3. Make all funeral arrangements and attend to burial of deceased.

4. Locate all bank accounts of deceased. Obtain information respecting amount payable on each. Notify the insurer of the death.

5. Locate all insurance policies, annuities, etc., and obtain information respecting amount payable on each. Notify the insurer of the death.

6. Notify pension offices of death.

7. List the contents of deceased's safety deposit box.

8. Completely review all personal papers of the deceased in order to locate all assets and debts.

9. Prepare a detailed inventory of deceased's assets and debts.

10. Arrange for storage of any assets requiring same. Advise insurers of any physical assets of the deceased. Arrange any insurance coverage required.

11. Notify the beneficiaries of the death and send them a Notice of an Application for a Certificate of Appointment of Estate Trustee.

12. Arrange with post office for mail to be re-addressed, if necessary.

13. Cancel any subscriptions or charge accounts. Return or destroy charge cards.

14. Obtain any "instant cash" required from banks, insurance companies, or employer.

15. Obtain all unpaid wages and other benefits from former employer.

16. Apply to court for Certificate of Appointment of Estate Trustee and pay all probate fees.

17. Reimburse for necessary and reasonable expenditures.

18. Advertise for creditors, if necessary.

19. File income tax return for year of death and any former years not yet filed by deceased.

20. Apply for Canada Pension Plan benefits, if any.

21. Apply for civil service, union, and/or veteran's benefits.

22. Apply for the balance of any amounts payable under insurance policies.

23. Sell any estate assets which must be sold or which personal representative chooses to sell (if he or she has the power).

24. Pay funeral expenses, income taxes payable, and all debts of deceased.

25. Pay money bequests and distribute other property in accordance with instructions in the will (being sure to retain sufficient cash to carry out the final steps).

26. Transfer or cancel insurance on house, car, etc.

27. File the estate's income tax returns and pay any tax owing. Issue any T-3 slips to beneficiaries.

28. Pay legal fees and any outstanding fees relating to the administration of the estate, including personal representative's compensation.

29. Obtain releases from all beneficiaries or pass estate accounts before a judge of the Superior Court of Justice.

30. Distribute the balance of the estate assets to the rightful beneficiaries.

GLOSSARY

ADMINISTRATOR

Individual appointed by the court to administer the estate of a person who dies without a will (feminine form "administratrix"). Also referred to as an estate trustee.

BENEFICIARY

Name given to a person who receives some benefit, whether money or property, from the will of a deceased person.

CAPITAL GAIN

Profit earned on the sale of an asset or profit deemed to be realized on the death of an individual, as if the asset had been sold on the date of death.

CAPITAL LOSS

Loss experienced on the sale of an asset or loss deemed to be experienced on the death of an individual, as if the asset had been sold on the date of death.

CERTIFICATE OF APPOINTMENT OF ESTATE TRUSTEE WITH A WILL

The term used by the Ontario Court for the court grant confirming the appointment of an estate trustee or executor named in the will and confirming the validity of the will itself.

CERTIFICATE OF APPOINTMENT OF ESTATE TRUSTEE WITHOUT A WILL

The term used by the Ontario Court for the court grant appointing an estate trustee to administer the estate of an individual dying intestate.

CODICIL

A document that makes a change or addition to a will requiring all the formalities of execution needed for a will.

ENCROACH

Act of paying out to the beneficiary portions of the money or other assets being held for that beneficiary in trust.

ESCHEAT

Process by which the assets of a deceased pass to the provincial government when he or she dies without a will and without a spouse or next-of-kin.

ESTATE TRUSTEE

Individual appointed in a will to administer the estate of the deceased or, where there is no will, an individual who applies for and is granted a Certificate of Appointment of Estate Trustee. Also referred to as a personal representative.

EXECUTOR

Individual appointed in a will to administer the estate of the deceased (feminine form "executrix"). Also referred to as a personal representative or an estate trustee.

HOLOGRAPH WILL

Will written completely in the handwriting of the person making it, having no witnesses to the signature of the testator; valid type of will in Ontario provided dated on or after March 31, 1978.

INTESTATE

Either the act of dying without a will or the person who dies without a will.

LIFE INTEREST

Benefit given to a beneficiary in a will which permits that beneficiary to have the use of some property or some amount of money for the balance of the beneficiary's lifetime only.

NEXT-OF-KIN

Blood relatives of a person dying intestate who inherit by reason of the .

NOTARIAL COPY

True copy of an original document, certified by a lawyer or notary public as being a true copy.

ONTARIO COURT (GENERAL DIVISION)

A branch of this court is responsible for the appointment of personal representatives and generally involved with problems arising during the administration of estates.

PERSONAL PROPERTY

All property with the exception of real estate and buildings (also known as "personalty").

PERSONAL REPRESENTATIVE

Name given to the individual administrating an estate, whether he or she be an administrator or an executor.

PER STIRPES

A method of dividing assets of an estate so that if a member of the group among which the assets are being divided happens to be dead at the time of the division, the children of that deceased member of the group will divide among them the share that their parent would have received had he or she been alive.

REAL PROPERTY

Land and buildings (also known as "real estate" and "realty").

RESIDUE

That portion of an estate remaining after all specific bequests and specific devises have been made.

RESIDUARY BENEFICIARY

Beneficiary to whom the residue of the estate is left.

SPECIFIC BEQUEST

Gift under a will of a specific item of personal property or a specific amount of cash.

SPECIFIC DEVISE

Gift under a will of a specific item of real property.

SUCCESSION LAW REFORM ACT

The Ontario legislation concerning wills, distribution on an intestacy, and support obligations on death.

TESTATE

The act of dying with a will.

TESTATOR

The name given to a man who makes a will (feminine form "testatrix").